Student Guide and Workbook
for

Social Work Skills Demonstrated
CD-ROM

Student Guide and Workbook
for

Social Work Skills Demonstrated
Beginning Direct Practice CD-ROM

Judith Sevel
Illinois State University

Linda Cummins

Cesar Madrigal

Allyn and Bacon
Boston · London · Toronto · Sydney · Tokyo · Singapore

Social Work Skills Demonstrated:
Beginning Direct Practice
Student Guide and Workbook
Table of Contents

System Requirements

PC Platform:

minimum	recommended
Windows 95 or NT	Windows 95 or NT
CPU:486/120Mhz	CPU: Pentium 166
Memory: 16Mb RAM	Memory: 32Mb RAM
CD-ROM Drive (2x)	CD-ROM Drive (4x)
Video: VGA/256 Colors	Video: VGA/16bit color
Sound Card (8 bit)	Sound Card (16 bit)

Macintosh Platform:

minimum	recommended
Macintosh System 7.x	Macintosh System 8.x
CPU: PPC or 68040	CPU: Power PC
Memory: 8Mb RAM	Memory: 16Mb RAM
CD-ROM Drive (2x)	CD-ROM Drive (4x)
Video: VGA/256 Colors	Video: VGA/1000's colors

Start Up

Step 1
To run Social Work Skills Demonstrated: Beginning Direct Practice, place the CD into the CD-ROM drive of your computer. After insertion, the CD should begin automatically. If it does not, double click on the CD-ROM icon located in the *My Computer* folder (for PCs).

Step 2
After double clicking on the CD-ROM icon, this screen will appear. Scroll until the icon called **Social** appears. Double click the **Social** icon to start the program.

Installing Quicktime

Step 1

If the *Media Check* window appears, your computer does not have the QuickTime version necessary to display the digital videos included in the Social Work CD. To install the correct version of QuickTime click **Yes**.

Step 2

Click the button labled **Yes** to begin installation.

Step 3

After clicking **Yes**, the QuickTime installer will automatically begin. Click **Next** to continue the installation.

Step 4

An informational screen now appears. Click **Next**.

Step 5

The next screen in the installation process asks you to accept the licesensing agreement. Click **Yes**.

Step 6

This screen gives you a choice of installations. To ensure installation of all necessary components, choose *full install*. Select **Next** to continue.

Step 7

If you would like to install the Quicktime Web browser plug-in, check the box(es) next to the names of the web browsers installed on your machine. To continue the installation process, click **Next**.

Step 8

This screen displays the folder name in which Quicktime will be installed. It does not need to be modified. To continue the install process, click **Next**.

Step 9

Click **Finish** to complete the QuickTime installation.

Step 10

Select the **Later** button to continue.

E-mail Settings

For the e-mail feature to function properly you must enter your SMTP server name (ask your Internet provider for this) and your return address.

Step 1

To access the settings screen, click on the **Links** button found in the main menu of Social Work Skills Demonstrated: Beginning Direct Pratice.

Step 2

After you open the links section of the CD, click on **Settings**. After clicking the settings button, enter your information. Then click **Save**.

> Your SMTP server   Save
> 111.11.11.1
> Your Name
> John Doe
> Your Email address
> jdoe@myaddress.com

Step 3

After clicking the **Save** button in the settings window click the **Links** button in the main menu. This will refresh the new e-mail settings that were entered. You may now e-mail the contents of the Links text area by entering an e-mail address in the **e-mail to:** field, and clicking the **Send** button.

> quiz
> links
> notes

> links/note taking
> web links: http://www.cswe.org
>   http://www.naswdc.org
>   http://www.ABacon.com/socwk/swhome.html
> email to: jberge@ilstu.edu   Send Mail
> settings   save mail   open file   print notes

Feature Information

Digital videos in the various program sections are controlled by the movie control bar. The bar performs the following functions:

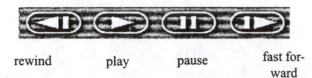

| rewind | play | pause | fast for-ward |

Notes

The Notes feature is accessible from the main menu, under **Notes**. The notes window allows you to take notes while the other sections of the program are running. Any text entered in the notepad is transferred to the **Links** text area, where it can be saved, printed, or emailed. Also, any text entered in the **Links** section will be visible from the **Notes** window.

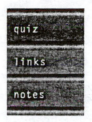

Student Guide and Workbook
for

Social Work Skills Demonstrated
CD-ROM

Chapter 1
An Introduction to Social Work

DEFINING SOCIAL WORK

Social work is the art and science of helping others. The field has a long tradition of helping the disadvantaged and influencing social policy to meet the dynamic continuum of human need. Social workers are represented in an array of professional positions, from the case-manager to the legislator. The profession is bound by common values and ethics that are grounded in respect for the individual and helping clients reach their potential by helping them function within the context of their environment. Whether it is a homeless person looking for shelter, a married couple addressing their differences, or an AIDS patient needing government assistance, social workers fulfill a variety of functions that meets the needs of others.

The National Association of Social Workers has put forward this defining statement:

> The purposes of both direct and indirect social work practice are to bring about the best possible adaptation among individuals, families, and groups and their environments; to set in motion a change process that will enhance people's problem-solving, coping, and developmental capacities; to link people with systems that provide resources, services, and opportunities; and to promote the effectiveness and humane operation of these systems. (National Association of Social Workers [NASW], 1981)

Fundamental social work principles are based on the assumption that people aspire to reach their full potential. The aim of social work is to create enriched environments that support individuals' optimal personal development, allowing them to hone their innate abilities within their social setting. As people are confronted with problems in life, their levels of coping and ability to adapt to current circumstances colors their perceptions of reality. How individuals interpret reality is correlated with levels of stress they experience in any given situation. For instance, a mother who views the challenges of toilet training her two year old as a normal developmental stage and major accomplishment for her child will approach the task with greater ease and excitement than a mother who interprets her child's inconsistency in toileting as defiant behavior. The latter mother sees her child as a problem while the first mother does not. Clearly, the mother who views toilet training as a normal part of her child's growth and development will be able to create a more supportive environment for the child to complete this critical task than the mother who sees the lack of bowel control in her two year old as a discipline problem.

From a social work perspective, both mothers are part of the environment that either enhances or deters their children's developmental potential. This interpretation springs from the *person-in-environment* perspective, a fundamental theory of social work practice that posits the continual interaction and shaping between individuals and their surroundings. The reciprocal nature of the relationship between individuals and their environments means that as individuals, we move and shape our surroundings, and that our surroundings have a profound effect on us as well. For instance, a mother who acknowledges and praises her child's mastery of toilet training affects the child's sense of competence and self-worth. As the child responds with pride in his or her accomplishment, the mother feels competence in her role as a mother. Both the mother and the child mutually shape their sense of well being. Conversely, the mother who sees toilet training as a discipline problem and responds with anger and punishment equally influences her child's sense of self worth. The child may respond with fear, confusion, and a feeling of inadequacy in meeting his or her mother's demands. The child's failure at toilet training may affirm the mother's suspicions of her own inadequacies as a parent. In both cases, the child and the mother mutually contribute to the stress or satisfaction they individually experience around the task of toilet training and the role of mothering.

Peoples' environments extend beyond their immediate family and encompass the entirety of their lived experiences, including interactions with extended families, friends, neighborhoods, schools, religious centers, public laws, cultural norms, and the economic system. To understand the complex interactions between individuals and all the components of their environment, social work draws upon *general systems theory* as a framework for understanding peoples problems and intervening in their lives. A system is defined as a whole made up of many interacting parts or subsystems (Ashford, Lecroy, & Lortie, 1997). For instance, a person represents an individual subsystem within a larger family system; a family is seen as a subsystem within a larger community system; and a community is a subsystem within a larger societal system. Social workers direct their attention to the total interactions among individuals and the sum of all social forces or systems (Haynes and Holmes, 1994) so that they may "promote or restore a mutually beneficial interaction between individuals and society in order to improve the quality of life"(NASW, 1997).

LEVELS OF PRACTICE

Optimal functioning of an individual in the environment requires subsystems that are also functioning at an optimal level, which promote individuals' development toward self-actualization. Dysfunction, individual or system functioning that limits or deters from reaching innate potentials can occur at the individual, family, community, organizational or societal level. Regardless of where the dysfunction originates within a system, it can create chaos that can be perpetuated throughout the associated subsystems. For example, a 14-year-old girl, Anna, who becomes pregnant, can affect not only her life, but also those around her. Anna's family can become quite distressed, react angrily, and expel her from their home, leaving her to fend for herself. Confused and alone, Anna may drop out of school in order to pursue employment to financially support herself. As an outcome of limited education, she seriously impairs her abilities to become self-sufficient and to support her child in the future. The employment and wage system is geared toward promoting people with education and skills, and has few supports for young single parents without an adequate education. The baby that Anna will give birth to will also face many challenges, such as poverty and under-nutrition, which in turn have a direct impact on the child's physical, mental, and psychological growth and development. Cultural norms that support a traditional family structure may negatively affect the psychological well being of both Anna and her child as they understand themselves to be outside the norms of their family and community. The social worker at the level of direct practice will work with Anna at a variety of levels in order to restore stability to her environmental system. The social worker may address 1) individual assessment and counseling with Anna; 2) reestablishing the girl's relationships with her family; 3) linking her to a prenatal care clinic and parenting classes; 4) connecting her to an educational program where she can complete her GED; 5) assisting her in an employment search; and, 6) applying for TANF and Medicaid welfare services.

The goal of direct practice is to assess and to improve the interaction of subsystems (the individual, family group, community, and organization) within the context of a larger societal system. The profession recognizes the importance of addressing systems at three levels. The **micro system** is the individual, and encompasses individuals' past history, experiences, unique personality, and accessibility to resources. The **mezzo system** is the small group, such as the family, which has its own complexities and dynamics. Such small groups strongly influence and are influenced by their individual members. The **macro system** is the large group, such as the societal institutions of work, schools, and the church (Zastrow, 1995). To this aim, Zastrow (1995) put forward four goals of social work practice that address all levels of system intervention:

1. Enhance people's problem-solving, coping, and developmental capacities;
2. Link people with systems that provide them with resources, services, and opportunities;
3. Promote the effective and humane operation of systems that provide people with resources and services; and
4. Develop and improve social policy (pp. 25-26).

Micro, mezzo, and macro systems interact along a continuum of healthy to unhealthy ways. The social worker interacts with systems at the micro, mezzo, and macro levels with the aim of enhancing system functioning so that healthy functioning dominates and dysfunction is minimized. This environment or ecology of systems plays an important part in the development of individual and family systems. Social work is at its best when the transactions of these systems promote growth and development of the individual, family, and community, and in exchange help make the environment amenable to positive growth among all the systems (Ashford, Lecroy, & Lortie, 1997). In the example of Anna above, the social worker intervenes at the **micro** level when involved in individual assessment and counseling with Anna; at the **mezzo** level when working with Anna's family, prenatal clinic, and parenting class; and, at the **macro** level when intervening with the educational, employment, and social welfare systems. Practice interventions at all three system levels are necessary to bringing stability to Anna's world.

THE HELPING PROCESS

Through direct practice, the social worker helps the client distinguish between healthy and unhealthy behaviors and ways of being. This can be a complex process, since many client problems and behaviors are long term, and have developed through the individual's interactions with multiple subsystems. For example, a 12-year-old boy with attention deficient hyperactivity disorder may present with behavior problems at home and in school, impaired academic performance, social isolation, and low self-esteem. At the micro or individual system, there are biological influences that affect the child's behavior problems that may need to be treated with medication. In the home (mezzo level) and at school (macro level) his behavior problems over time may have caused him to be isolated from peers. In addition, he may have been labeled as the "difficult child or student." His behavior problems at school may interfere with the learning process and consequently he is behind his peers in academic achievement. All of these problems collectively, over time, may have led the boy to conclude that he is in some way inadequate and contributed to his low self-esteem. The sorting out of the influences of different systems in the boy's life and deciding on appropriate interventions requires a significant amount of knowledge and skill on the part of the social worker.

Multiple interventions are often required to sufficiently alleviate the presenting and interconnected problems of clients. Social workers use the helping process, a problem-solving process, to guide them in structuring a plan of action aimed at improving the quality of life for their clients. For the helping process to be successful, the social worker must establish a partnership with the client that is grounded in mutual respect and trust. Together, the client and social worker identify mutual goals to be attained through the helping process. The social worker facilitates the helping process through the application of social work theory and skills. The social worker guides the client through the following five stages of the problem-solving or helping process.

The first stage of the helping process is *assessment*. During this stage the social worker gathers information from the client and other related systems that identify the client's problem(s) and the client's strengths (Germaine & Gitterman, 1995). When data collection is complete, the social worker then analyzes the interacting dynamics of the client's systems that have contributed to the presenting problem(s) as well as how the client's strengths can be used in resolving their problems (Haynes & Holmes, 1994). Assessment is not a static process but ongoing throughout the helping relationship.

When the social worker and the client have mutually agreed upon the problems to be addressed through the helping process, both move into the next phase, the *planning* stage. Setting goals and developing a plan of action are the essential components of the planning stage. Setting goals provides focus and direction to the helping process (Hepworth, Rooney, & Larsen, 1997), helps in identifying obstacles that need to be overcome by the client (Haynes & Holmes, 1994), and establishes a clearer vision of life's possibilities for the client. Together, the social worker and client develop specific strategies for attaining the mutually determined goals of the helping relationship. During this stage the social worker and client develop a detailed contract defining the long- and short-term goals and the specific tasks to be completed within a designated time period. The social worker–client contract can be written or verbal. The contract functions to provide a means of accountability, for monitoring client progress, and to determine when termination of the helping relationship is appropriate (Hepworth, Rooney, & Larsen, 1997).

After the social worker and client have agreed to a plan of action, fulfilling the agreement occurs during the *implementation* stage. Successful implementation requires a goal-oriented interaction between the social worker and client. Both parties are accountable for completing specific tasks agreed to within the contract. Tasks may be directed toward the client's individual issues or may be related to other resource systems (Hepworth, Rooney, & Larsen, 1997).

Together the social worker and client carry out the mutually agreed upon plan of action. In doing so the client and social worker take on specific roles. Roles are defined as the particular obligations and expectations that both have accepted as an outcome of the social worker–client contract (Zastrow & Kirst-Ashman, 1997). For example, a client presenting with the problem of unemployment due to a work-related injury requires the social worker to be a broker of services. Expectations of this role may include the social worker seeking out training programs for reemployment, workers' compensation benefits, and transportation and childcare for the client if needed. Additionally, the social worker would take on the role of counselor and would provide emotional support as the client works through his or her issues of loss related to injury and job displacement. Client roles would include following up on employment leads, completing necessary paper work for workers' compensation benefits, seeking out child care from friends and relatives, and exploring education and training opportunities. Successful implementation occurs in the context of a social worker–client relationship that is imbued with trust, a belief that change is possible, and a commitment to fulfilling the role expectations as defined by the contract (Hepworth, Rooney, & Larsen, 1997).

Evaluation assesses the extent to which the goals set forth by the client and social worker have been attained through the helping process. Has the process been effective in resolving the presenting problem (Sheafor, Horejsi, & Horejsi, 1997)? It is through the evaluation process that the social worker and client come to a conclusion about the effectiveness of the helping relationship. Based on that conclusion, they will mutually decide if the relationship continues, is renegotiated, or terminated. If the goals set forth at the beginning of the helping process remain relevant to the client's progress, the relationship would most likely continue. If the client's circumstances have changed and the goals are no longer relevant, the contract may be renegotiated. If the goals have been attained and the presenting problem resolved, the relationships would be terminated. Evaluation is an ongoing process that occurs periodically throughout the helping relationship.

Termination, the final stage of the helping relationship, is the process of mutually determining when and how the helping relationship will end. Optimally, termination is a planned process that begins at the outset of the helping relationship. One of the cornerstones of social work is client self-determination and empowerment. The client and social worker come to a decision about termination by examining the client's willingness and ability to make healthy life decisions for him or herself and confidently follow through and act on those decisions. A critical phase of the termination process is a review of the client's progress in moving toward established goals as identified in the social worker–client contract. In the review process the social worker considers the client's ability to problem solve independently; willingness to access available resources when problems arise in the future; and commitment to maintaining the progress made throughout the helping process. As the social worker and client engage in problem solving throughout the helping relationship, they are, in fact, preparing for termination. The helping relationship provides the client with the steps of problem solving, and a repertoire of skills for successfully navigating life's problems beyond the helping relationship.

The helping process is a fluid and dynamic sequence of social worker–client interactions directed toward problem resolution and growth. The stages of the helping process are not discrete, but build on one another as the helping relationship evolves. Neither are they strictly linear, as the social worker assesses the client situation, evaluates the client's progress and introduces new interventions as the relationship unfolds. Box 1.1 demonstrates the dynamic and complex nature of the helping relationship.

Box 1.1

You are a social worker at a not-for-profit social service agency that provides support services and training to help young single mothers achieve self-sufficiency. Sarah, a 17-year-old single pregnant female was referred to your agency by her school counselor. At intake Sarah's *presenting problem* is that of impending homelessness. She is four months pregnant and has been kicked out of her parent's home. She's confused and depressed and uncertain about how to handle her situation. During the *assessment* process, you discover that Sarah is without family support, has dropped out of school, isolated herself from her peers, and has no money or any place to live. Although fearful, Sarah has been a responsible student and daughter, is motivated to establish some stability in her life and is seeking help in improving her situation. Together you and Sarah identify problem areas that need to be addressed and accentuate her strengths in constructing a *plan of action* and *contract*. The following treatment goals were mutually agreed upon:
1) access to prenatal care; 2) apply for Medicaid and TANF; 3) explore temporary housing and apply for subsidized housing benefits; 4) enroll in single parent support group; 5) ongoing individual counseling for dealing with issues of family disruption, self-esteem, and depression; 6) enrollment in GED classes; 7) vocational training for job placement; and 8) beginning parenting classes and family planning soon after the birth of her child. Together you and Sarah prioritized the treatment goals and placed them within a specific time frame. During the *implementation stage,* Sarah was able to find temporary housing with a family friend until the birth of her child. Meanwhile, as her social worker you linked her to a local public health clinic where she received prenatal care, and referred her to the public aid office where she applied for and received Medicaid and TANF benefit.
2) Sarah attended her GED classes twice a week and planned on completing her diploma by the time her child is born. In addition, you referred her to the local housing authority where Sarah applied for subsidized housing. At the time she was facing a waiting list of six months. Sarah continued her weekly counseling session and was able to begin to consider mending her broken relationships with her parents. Sarah enrolled in early childhood development training program in preparation for employment after the birth of her child. Classes will begin when she completes her GED program. After six months of working with Sarah as her primary social worker, you *evaluate*d her progress and assessed the extent to which she had been able to attain her treatment goals. Over the five-month period, Sarah made the following progress on her treatment goals: 1) consistently kept her prenatal care appointments, followed her physicians instructions, and gave birth to a full-term, healthy son; 2) received Medicaid and TANF benefits and maintained her eligibility; 3) moved into a one-bedroom public housing unit in a safe neighborhood; 4) attended only two sessions of her single-parent support group; 5) attended 90 percent of her weekly counseling sessions and was feeling more focused and less depressed; 6) reestablished communication with her family; 7) completed her GED; 8) was scheduled to begin child care development classes in six

Box 1.1, con't.

weeks; 9) had information on the local family planning clinic; and 10) received in-home parenting instruction from a home interventionist working with new mothers. Together, you and Sarah conclude that Sarah has acquired a sufficient level of empowerment and determine that it is time to *terminate* the helping relationship. You and Sarah have created an environmental structure that will support and nurture her and her son, and as her social worker, you leave the door open for future contact.

SOCIAL WORKER ROLES

When effectively navigating the helping process, social workers take on a variety of roles that facilitate client change (see Box 1.2). Role is defined as expected professional behaviors and functions accepted by the social work profession, and frequently employed in social work practice (Zastrow & Kirst-Ashman, 1997). Over the course of a career, a social worker may play several or all of the social worker roles and over time will develop competency in most of the roles. Several factors influence which roles a social worker will play, such as the goals of the agency where one is employed; the latitude of the social worker's responsibilities in a given work setting; the needs of the client; and one's level of practice (see Box 1.2). The social worker's roles may be restricted to one level of practice, or may encompass all three levels (micro, mezzo, and macro). Roles will shift when the responsibilities of the social worker move across levels of practice (see Box 1.3). For example, as the social worker in the scenario presented in Box 1.1 you were required to practice at the micro and mezzo levels in order to serve the best interests of your client. At the micro level, the social worker took on the roles of *enabler* and *counselor*. At the mezzo level the social worker acted as a *broker* where she connected Sarah to community resources (prenatal care, single parent support group; GED classes, vocational training, parenting classes, Medicaid and TANF benefits, housing assistance, and family planning). The social worker also played the role of *mediator* (mezzo) in resolving the conflict between Sarah and her parents. If there had been no parenting classes available in Sarah's community, the social worker could have taken of the role of *initiator* (macro), and developed a parenting class for Sarah and other expectant mothers to attend in their community.

Box 1.2

Social Work Roles

Enabler: the social worker offers support and encouragement to clients so that they can more easily accomplish tasks and solve problems; for example, helping a mental health patient adjust to day treatment.

Mediator: the social worker takes a neutral stance between two systems in order to help resolve conflict and to help establish better communications flow; for example, divorce mediation.

Counselor: the social worker helps improve client functioning by helping them gain insights into feelings, change behaviors and acquires problem solving skills;

Broker: the social worker connects the client to needed resources; for example, a

Box 1.2, con't.

client recently diagnosed as HIV-positive. The social worker investigates various medical and supportive services and assesses them in light of the client's insurance coverage and available financial resources.

Advocate: the social worker champions the rights of others through empowerment or direct intervention. For example, a person who became recently disabled was fired from his job, although still able
to do the work. The social worker assists the client in pursuing legal recourse.

Facilitator: the social worker leads a group, such as a rape survivors' recovery group.

General manager: the social worker is an agency administrator.

Educator: the social worker teaches others at the individual or group level; for example, teaching a client job search skills, or teaching a group of expectant mothers prenatal classes;

Researcher/program evaluator: the social worker evaluates program effectiveness; for example, the effectiveness of a community health agency in meeting community needs.

Initiator: the social worker develops programs, such as a school for deaf children in the community.

Integrator/ coordinator: the social worker helps a variety of systems to work together at fulfilling goals; for example, working with police departments, schools, and parents in developing community drug awareness programs.

Level of Practice	Social Work Role
Micro	enabler; counselor; educator
Mezzo	mediator; broker; facilitator; general manager; educator; research/program evaluator; initiator
Macro	broker; advocate; initiator; integrator/coordinator

(Sheafor, Horejsi, & Horejsi, 1997; Zastrow & Kirst-Ashman, 1997)

Given the complexity of the social service system, and the unpredictability of the human experience, social workers often have ethical and moral obligations to serve in multiple roles across all levels of practice if client needs are to be sufficiently met. Further, the *person-in-environment* perspective mandates that the individual's problem be understood in the context of systems at various levels. The multidimensional nature of social work makes it unlikely that a direct practice social worker could restrict the social worker roles to one or two roles, or limit his or her practice to only one level. All social worker roles serve to move us in the direction of social justice by improving quality of life and structuring supportive environments at the family, community, organizational, and institutional levels.

Regardless of the roles you fill as a direct practice social worker, you will need interviewing skills to master the roles and meet the needs of your clients. Experienced social workers realize that interviewing is a skill that must be sharpened continually, and that it has an important place in direct practice at the micro, mezzo, and macro levels. Each new client has a story to tell, whether the client is an individual, family, community, or organization. The social worker must elicit and understand that story in order to be an effective helper. The skills that are explained in the following chapters cannot be learned in a single semester. Think of them instead as a career's work—and this CD-ROM, manual, and accompanying workbook are your first steps toward mastery.

FOR FURTHER READING

Gambril, E. (1997). *Social work practice*. Oxford: Oxford University Press.

Murphy, B. & Dillon, C. (1998). *Interviewing in action*. Pacific Grove, CA: Brooks/Cole.

Sheafor, B., Horejsi, C. & Horejsi, G. (1997). *Techniques and guidelines for social work practice*, 4th ed. Boston, MA: Allyn & Bacon.

Gordon, R. (1992). *Basic interviewing skills*. Itasca, IL: Peacock.

Chapter 2
Values and Ethics in Social Work

Social work is a practice-oriented profession grounded in the core values of self-determination, empowerment, confidentiality, and a belief in the inherent worth and dignity of all human beings. As practitioners, social workers are involved in the lives of people facing difficult and trying problems and circumstances. The actions social workers take in the course of practice have a direct impact on the quality of life for their clients. When working with troubled individuals, we can just as easily add to the hardships of clients' lives, if our professional actions are not grounded in the values of the profession and guided by the mission of the profession. It is therefore essential that social workers be self-conscious about the possible outcomes of their interactions with clients.

Social work values are idealistic and difficult to sustain in our human condition. To be a social worker requires that you aspire to the values and mission of the profession, that you strive to derive your actions from them in your professional life, and that you recommit to them everyday. Social work values guide the profession toward the fulfillment of its mission of social justice, whose goal is that all members of society have equal access to resources sufficient for a healthy and supportive environment. It is important that individual social work practitioners understand the nature of social work values and incorporate them into their daily practice with clients.

Social work practice can take many forms. At the micro level, social workers work with clients as individuals, in families, or in groups, in public, not-for-profit, or private agencies. At the mezzo level of practice, social workers may find themselves involved in program and policy development or research evaluation within community agencies or private corporations. On the macro level, social workers may be involved with community organizing and development, or working in the political arena as a state or federal employee, elected official, policy analyst, or lobbyist. Regardless of the setting of your social work practice, consideration must be given to how, as individual social work practitioners, we personify the values of the profession. Social work values are exhibited in how we relate to clients, how service delivery systems are structured, and how, as social workers, we serve as a political voice of disadvantaged and marginalized people in society.

In most introductory skills courses, and in this CD-ROM, the focus of practice is on the individual client. Keep in mind however, that social work values infuse every level of practice, whether at the individual level or at the level of policymaking.

SOCIAL WORK MISSION

Ultimately, the purpose of social work is to advance the quality of life for all people through the enhancement of mutually beneficial interactions between individuals and society (Minahan, 1981). Social work stands for the social welfare of all people and is committed to social justice through social change at the individual, family, community, agency, and structural levels. As such, social work has historically been and continues to be in alliance with those members of society who live under oppressive conditions that keep them disadvantaged and marginalized. The profession of social work envisions a more decent and humane society (Ehrenreich, 1985).

Unique to social work as a helping profession is the *person in environment perspective*, which is based on the idea that one can not understand the problems of individuals without understanding the context in which they occur. The context, or environment, encompasses the individual's perceptions of self, family roles and conditions, community supports, agency functioning in meeting the individual's needs, and the interactions between the individual and societal institutions such as economic, political, educational, religious, family, and social welfare systems. Social work, then, has a dual focus, enhancing individuals' functioning in society by empowering them to achieve life goals, and pursuing social changes that are likely to provide a supportive environment for all members of society (Reamer, 1997a). Supportive environments give individuals access to opportunities and resources within all the institutions in society, without regard for irrelevant attributes such as age, race, gender, religious or political affiliation, or sexual orientation. In doing so, disadvantaged individuals and groups have equal access to mainstream institutions that provide education, employment, wages, housing, nutrition, social supports, and health care. Equal access to these basic resources can alleviate distress and suffering.

Opportunities to contribute to society are essential to one's well being. Ultimately, we as human beings are created for the purpose of expressing the innate talents that we possess at birth. Without opportunities for self-expression, human beings become withdrawn, fearful, and weighted down by a sense of having little worth. Social work supports the notion that people should be treated humanely and that transactions between individuals and the environment should enhance one's dignity, feelings of self-worth, and full self-expression (Haynes & Holmes, 1994). The mission of social work rests on professional values that ennoble men and women, and call forth their greatest being (Ehrenreich, 1985).

SOCIAL WORK VALUES

Social work values support the mission of social work and guide the profession in creating a humane vision of the world. The social work vision calls for individuals, regardless of their beliefs, practices, or backgrounds, to be treated with dignity, given equal access to societal institutions, opportunities and resources, and supported in contributing their unique talents to their families, communities, and country. At a fundamental level, social work values are congruent with and supportive of the values and beliefs reflected in the Declaration of Independence—that all are created equal and endowed with certain inalienable rights such as life, liberty, and the pursuit of happiness (Haynes & Holmes, 1994). And much like the visionaries who crafted the Declaration of Independence, social workers belong to a profession of action and passion in advocating for the downtrodden; they stand for social justice and human decency (Ehrenreich, 1985). However, for the passion of the profession's values to come alive, they must be put into action; that is, incorporated into one's way of being. Helen Harris Perlman (1976) captured this concept best when she wrote, "A value has small worth except as it is moved, or is moveable, from believing into doing, from verbal affirmation into action" (p.381). Social work practitioners, then, must relate to clients in a way that preserves or enhances their dignity and self-worth. They must structure services in a manner that gives equal access to resources, and support policies that reflect the belief in a just society and the belief that change is possible in individuals, communities, and organizations (Haynes & Holmes, 1994; Reamer, 1995). Only when we have moved social work values from the abstract ideal into empowering action in our professional lives can we claim them as our own (Reamer, 1995). Social work practice is the application of social work values to helping relationships with clients, groups, communities, organizations, and other professionals (Zastrow, 1995).

Self-Determination

Self-determination is the act of giving clients the freedom to make choices in their lives and to move toward their established goals in a manner that they see as most fitting for them, so long as clients' choices don't infringe on the rights of others (Zastrow, 1995). As social workers, we may not agree with our clients' choices, but supporting self-determination requires that we respect our clients in their life choices, whether or not we agree with them. Our job as social workers is not to tell clients what to do or what not to do, but rather to explore options with the client and the possible outcome of life choices (Haynes & Holmes, 1994). Often, we may experience conflicts between our personal value base and that of the client (see Box 2.1).

Box 2.1

Self-Determination and Personal Value Conflicts

You are a drug and alcohol counselor employed at an outpatient treatment center. Susan is a new client of yours who was referred by her employer for alcohol treatment after having repeated "hangover" mornings at work. Recently she appeared at work fully intoxicated. Susan is an architect at a local firm, married, and the mother of two daughters, ages 12 and 14 years. During your third session with Susan, she mentions that she is having an affair. By the sixth session, you learn that Susan has had a series of affairs throughout her 16-year marriage, and that it is a common practice of Susan's to introduce her daughters to her lovers. Susan does not seem troubled by her extra-marital affairs, and does not ask you for any help in this area of her life.

You are also married with children, but adhere to the middle-class traditional family values of monogamy, and honest and open communications in your marital relationship. You find Susan's behavior quite disturbing.

1. Are the value conflicts inherent in your relationship with Susan personal or professional?
2. How relevant are Susan's extra-marital affairs to her alcohol problem and recovery program?
3. As a social worker committed to client self-determination, how would you proceed in your professional relationship with Susan?

(Reamer, 1995)

Since it is the client's quality of life we are dedicated to enhancing, we must first and foremost allow the client's values to dominate. This is much easier said than done when we are confronted with client values and behaviors that contradict our own ideals for living a moral life. We often struggle with the desire to impose our values on our clients in practice situations. All people are strongly attached to their personal value system. It is the base from which all our opinions and behaviors emanate. As social workers, we must give up the notion that our personal value system is the model that our clients should follow. We may prefer our personal value system to that of our clients, but it may not be necessarily a better value system, only different. For clients to be self-determining, it is essential that they be permitted to live within their own value system. Self-determination enhances clients' abilities to help themselves and fosters self-reliance and self-sufficiency. As we cede them the power to make decisions in their lives, we also cede them the responsibility that goes with decision making and the outcomes of those decisions. When we support clients through the self-determination process we help create an avenue for clients' expressions of their inherent worth and dignity (Zastrow, 1995).

Empowerment

Empowerment lays the groundwork for informed self-determination. Although social workers provide opportunities for empowerment, only clients can empower themselves (the desire to change must originate within the client for it to be genuine). Through thoughtful decision making, clients move themselves toward their goals. Social workers assist in this process by providing information, assisting the client in building support systems, and exploring possible outcomes of various life choices. Social workers guide clients to a position where they can make informed choices about their lives. On the surface, empowerment sounds like a fairly simple, yet ideal process. In reality, creating empowering options for clients whose behaviors violate our personal sense of what is right and wrong can be challenging at best.

Box 2.2

Creating Empowering Options

As a case manager at the local Housing Authority office, you are responsible for helping low-income families gain access to safe, affordable, and when eligible, subsidized housing. Judy is a 30-year-old single mother of two who has been on welfare assistance for three years. For two years, Judy and her family drifted in and out of homelessness when her unstable housing arrangements fell apart. You have been working with Judy in finding her stable housing for 18 months. After being on the waiting list for public housing for a full year, you were able to help Judy secure a two-bedroom apartment in a housing project designated for young families that is located in a safe neighborhood. Judy and her family have been in their new apartment for six months, and for the first time in their young lives, her children are experiencing what it means to have a stable home. This afternoon, you received a call from the local police informing you that Judy has been arrested for drug trafficking in her apartment. The Housing Authority's policy forbids the use or selling of drugs in public housing units, and requires that residents who violate this rule be evicted immediately.

1. Given your agency responsibility with the Housing Authority, what empowering options can you create for your client, Judy?
2. Do you see any value conflicts between the agency's drug policy and social work values? If so, what are they?
3. When you go to the jail to visit Judy, what will you say to her?

Inherent Worth and Dignity

A core value of the social work profession is respect for every human being's innate greatness. Social workers are trained to regard clients as having worth and to treat them with dignity, regardless of their outward behaviors. It is our job as social workers to provide the supportive environment for the client to fully express that innate greatness. In doing so, we create a process of affirmation that over time generates a growing sense of self-worth in the client.

To put into action the value of inherent worth and dignity, the social worker must be able to view people as unique individuals, and not impose preconceived notions, or stereotypes, on people possessing certain characteristic (see Box 2.3). This is the process of individualization (Zastrow, 1995), of knowing people for themselves, instead of "knowing" people through the distortions of our own biases.

Box 2.3

> ### Stereotyping versus Individualization
> Consider your initial impressions and assumptions about the following types of clients that you may encounter in your practice. Write them down and then identify what is true for everyone with a particular characteristic; identify your beliefs that are based on stereotypes you've learned in your experiences and socialization.
>
> **1. An African American welfare mother;**
> **2. A homeless teenager of Mexican descent alone on the streets;**
> **3. A 24-year-old white male with AIDS.**
>
> The only indisputable things we can say about the potential clients described above is that you would be working with a poor African American mother, a Mexican teenager who has no home, and a young white male infected with AIDS. What other assumptions did you make about your potential clients? Consider where your impressions came from and the types of values reflected in your assumptions. Through honest self-reflection, we can begin to let go of our stereotypes, and move toward individualization and the possibility of knowing our clients as unique individuals.

Respecting people for their inherent worth and dignity also requires social workers to be willing and able to separate individuals' behaviors from who they are inherently as human beings. When our clients adhere to values, lifestyles, and behavior patterns that are similar to our own, relating to our clients with unconditional regard is easy to do. However, when a client's behaviors are at odds with our personal value system, engaging the client with unconditional regard can be very difficult (see Box 2.4).

Box 2.4

> ### Separating Client Behaviors from the Client
> Consider your reactions to the following clients. How difficult would it be for you to view these clients with respect? Identify the values and emotions that limit your ability to relate to these clients with unconditional regard.

Box 2.4, con't.

1. A 35-year-old father who has sexually abused his six-year-old daughter;
2. A 15-year-old girl who shot and killed her mother while she slept;
3. A 45-year-old man arrested for selling drugs to grade-school children;
4. A 30-year-old single mother who left her three-year-old daughter locked in her room for a weekend while she went away with her boyfriend.

Zastrow (1995) offers two guidelines for working with clients whose behaviors appall and disgust us. First, accept that the individual and their behaviors can be separated. In doing so, you create an opening for treating clients with respect and viewing them as capable of change. By separating the behavior from the person, you can give yourself permission to despise the behavior without disrespecting the person. Second, recognize that with some clients, it will be difficult if not impossible for you to get past the heinousness of their behavior and treat them with the respect that is needed in order to establish a helping relationship. When this occurs, and it happens for almost all social workers at some point in their practice careers, it is in the best interest of the client to transfer the case to another social worker. If you cannot conceive of the client as having innate greatness and inherent worth and dignity, a helping relationship cannot be created.

All people are inherently great; it's just that some have forgotten. When we forget who we are innately, we become disconnected from ourselves, and express who we are *not,* through destructive behaviors. When we can stand in the possibility of our client's greatness, we have transcended our own biases and made an empathic connection with them. Only then can we effectively enter into our client's world and their lived experiences (Haynes & Holmes, 1994). The role of the social worker is to help individuals remember who they are, innately, and support them in expressing their greatness. Often this is unfamiliar territory, and clients will need a great deal of support, encouragement, and affirmation to engage in ways of being that have, to this point in their lives, been foreign to them. To stay in this process with the client requires us to acknowledge and draw upon our own innate greatness, and to have compassion for our clients when they fail, and for ourselves when we fail to stay in our commitment to our client's ability to change and create a better life. Social work practice requires an ongoing recommitment to the mission of our profession, the values that support it, and our clients' inherent worth and dignity.

Confidentiality

Confidentiality refers to the safeguarding of the information that passes between the social worker and the client. This aspect of the social worker–client relationship facilitates the evolution of a trusting relationship that is essential for client change. Trusting that what transpires during the interview session will remain private, clients can begin to express their concerns and aspirations within a safe environment. Once that occurs, the social worker can obtain the necessary information to create empowering options for clients and support them in their life choices. It also creates a supportive environment in which clients can begin to express their innate goodness.

State laws, the NASW code of ethics, and certain agency policies impose limitations on confidentiality within the social worker–client relationship. The NASW code of ethics and some state laws require that social workers report to the appropriate authorities clients' intentions to harm another individual or themselves. All states require that social workers report known or suspected cases of child abuse or neglect. Social service agencies that use a team treatment approach may require that all team members have access to pertinent information about the client. It is the ethical responsibility of the social worker to inform clients of the limits of confidentiality at the outset of the helping relationship (Gothard, 1997; NASW, 1997; Polowy & Gorenberg, 1997). However, even when we are knowledgeable about the legal and ethical limits of confidentiality, in the real practice world it is often difficult to identify when we have reached these limits within the helping relationship. Box 2.5 provides an example of this dilemma.

Box 2.5

A Confidentiality Issue

You are a caseworker at a Family Service Center, where you have worked for one month since receiving your BSW. Richard is a 48-year-old construction worker whom you have been seeing weekly since your first week at the agency. Richard came to your agency seeking assistance after unexpectedly losing his job following a back injury that left him permanently limited in his abilities to lift or carry more than five pounds, or to climb and do twisting motions. Richard is a devoted husband and father and is feeling that he has let his family down because he has not been able to provide for them financially in recent months. With your help, Richard has been able to enter an 8-week reemployment-training program where he is being trained as a tax preparer for a local firm. He has done well in his classes, but has become depressed and frustrated in the past two weeks as his family's financial situation has worsened. Today, you notice that Richard seems more agitated and restless. When you asked him what is on his mind, he explains that the previous night he had been out at the local tavern having a few beers and on the way home was stopped for speeding and was given a DWI when he failed to pass the Breathalyzer test. The ordeal resulted in Richard being held in jail overnight, causing him to miss his tax preparer's class the following morning. He is feeling unjustly persecuted by the police, and fears that he will not be permitted to complete the class. As Richard is telling you of the events of the previous evening, he becomes enraged at the unfortunate hand that fate has dealt him and blurts out, "I feel like walking into the police station and shooting those bastards!"

1. **How will you handle the issue of confidentiality in your relationship with Richard?**
2. **How do you determine whether Richard is serious about his threat or just venting his anger?**
3. **What actions would you take?**

SOCIAL WORK ETHICS

Social work ethics provide social work practitioners with a set of guidelines for practice. These guidelines are established by the National Association of Social Workers, the major professional social work organization, and reflect the values of the profession. Social work ethics translate the abstract values of the profession into action statements and give social workers concrete guidelines for ethical ways of being in the practice setting. The first code of ethics was adopted in 1960, and was later revised, in 1979 and 1996, to reflected the changing emphasis and direction of social work practice and changing social and political times (Haynes & Holmes, 1994; Reamer, 1997b). Box 2.6 summarizes the six ethical principles of the NASW Code of Ethics.

Box 2.6

Ethical Principles of the Social Work Profession
1. Social workers' primary goal is to help people in need and to address social problems;   2. Social workers challenge social injustice;   3. Social workers respect the inherent dignity and worth of the person;   4. Social workers recognize the central importance of human relationships;   5. Social workers behave in a trustworthy manner;   6. Social workers practice within their areas of competence and develop and enhance their professional expertise.   <div align="right">(NASW, 1997)</div>

Charles Levy (1976) notes that social work ethics serve three functions for the profession: "It guides a professional conduct, it is a set of principles that social workers can apply in the performance of the social work function, and it is a set of criteria by which social work practice can be evaluated." By understanding the established ethics of social work practice, social workers can make the difficult moral and value-laden decisions that that are inescapably part of working with people from diverse walks of life. Social workers who find themselves within practice settings that may not adhere to the values of the social work profession have a supportive and clear set of guidelines. Box 2.7 outlines the areas of social workers' ethical responsibilities that are addressed in the NASW Code of Ethics.

Box 2.7

Social Workers' Ethical Responsibilities
1. Social workers have ethical responsibilities to clients;   2. Social workers have ethical responsibilities to colleagues;   3. Social workers have ethical responsibilities in the practice setting;   4. Social workers have ethical responsibilities as professionals;   5. Social workers have ethical responsibilities to the social work profession;   6. Social workers have ethical responsibilities to the broader society.   <div align="right">(NASW, 1997)</div>

Ethical Dilemmas

The social work profession is sanctioned by society through the passage of public laws, and through the appropriation of public funds to fulfill the mandates of public law. Social work therefore has an obligation to society to provide services, counseling, and interventions for those in need. In this sense, the public at large shows support for the values and mission of social work. Public laws and regulations also direct social work practice in the sense that as social workers we are mandated by law to provide certain services, and to structure those services in predetermined ways. Often the values inherent in the public laws directing social work practice are in conflict with the values inherent in the social work practice. At times, this may put the social work practitioner in an ethical dilemma when trying to satisfy the demands of two competing value systems (see Box 2.8).

Box 2.8

Conflicting Values: Social Work and Social Policy

Let's return to the case of Sarah, presented in Chapter 1. Recall that you are a social worker at a not-for-profit social service agency that provides support services and training to help young single mothers achieve self-sufficiency. Over the past two years, you have seen Sarah intermittently. She has become one of your favorite clients, in part because of her perseverance and her willingness to follow through on her commitments. Sarah is now 19 years old; her son, Seth, is two. Since you began working with Sarah, she has attended parenting classes and proven herself to be a loving and skilled mother. She has also completed her GED. With the help of housing assistance, she has been able to secure a two-bedroom apartment after being on the waiting list for six months. Eight months ago, Sarah got her first real job as an assistant teacher in a daycare center, working 20 hours per week. Sarah likes her job very much, and she excels at her work. The job only pays $5.25 per hour and provides no health care or paid time-off benefits. However, as an employee of the daycare center, Sarah receives free daycare for her son Seth. With her TANF (Temporary Aid to Needy Families) income, food stamps, Medicaid, subsidized housing, part-time job, and free daycare, Sarah has managed to create a stable life for her son.

In the state where you practice, clients can only receive TANF benefits for two years. As you review Sarah's case file, you see that her welfare benefits will expire in one month. Sarah needs the welfare check to meet basic survival needs for herself and her son. If she budgets carefully, her welfare check and work income together just cover her rent, secondhand clothing for Seth, bus fare to work, the phone bill, and essential items like toothpaste and soap that are not covered by foodstamps. Without her welfare check, Sarah is likely to find herself in the same situation she was in two years earlier, homeless with her young son.

1. What social work value does the state TANF policy contradict?
2. As a social worker, how do you comply with state law without violating social work values?
3. What options can you present to Sarah that will be empowering to her and her son?

CONCLUSION

Social work as a profession is dedicated to social justice and the empowerment of all people through the creation of a just society where men and women are given equal access to resources and opportunities. These ideals often attract people to the profession who are committed to helping people. Putting social work values into practice is a continuing challenge, though, and not just for the new social worker. Staying focused on creating a society where all people enjoy a safe and supportive environment helps us through the difficult cases. Witnessing our clients' successes as they reconnect with their innate greatness and create stable and fulfilling lives is the priceless reward that social workers reap in direct social work practice.

FOR FURTHER READING

Ehrenreich, J. H. (1985). *The Altruistic Imagination.* Ithaca, NY: Cornell University Press.

Gothard, S. (1997). Legal issues: Confidentiality and privileged communication. *In* National Association of Social Workers *Encyclopedia of Social Work,* 19th ed. Washington, DC: NASW.

National Association of Social Workers (1997). *Encyclopedia of Social Work,* 19th ed. Washington, DC: NASW.

Perlman H. H. (1976). Believing and doing: Values in social work education. *Social Casework,* 7(6), 381-390.

Polowy, C. I. and Gorenberg, C. (1997). Legal issues: Recent developments in confidentiality and privilege. In National Association of Social Workers *Encyclopedia of Social Work,* 19th ed. Washington, DC: NASW.

Reamer, F.G. (1997a).Ethics and values. In National Association of Social Workers *Encyclopedia of Social Work,* 19th ed. Washington, DC: NASW.

Reamer, F.G. (1997b). Ethical standards in social work: The *NASW Code of Ethics.* In National Association of Social Workers *Encyclopedia of Social Work,* 19th ed. Washington, DC: NASW.

Chapter 3
Social Work Skills

For social workers, the key to working effectively with clients is developing expertise in the basic skills of communication. This pursuit involves formal academic education, professional training, supervision, and an overall commitment to *practice* social work skills. During the interview process the social worker connects with the client through the use of empathic responses such as reflection of feeling, paraphrasing, and attending behaviors. Using social work skills effectively requires more than just knowing the skill; the social worker must determine when it is appropriate to use the skill by gauging the client's likely response. This level of expertise takes considerable effort to develop, but it can be learned. Although social workers who are new to the field occasionally struggle to give the best response to a client, with practice, interviewing clients becomes an opportunity to put in to action the values of the social work profession. This chapter introduces the basic interviewing skills that are the first steps toward a career-long pursuit of excellence in the helping relationship.

INTERVIEWING SKILLS

Reflection of Feeling

Reflection of feeling, one of the most important skills in the social worker's repertoire, requires the social worker to restate and explore the client's affective (feeling) statements. Frequently, the client is experiencing a wide variety of feelings and has difficulty separating them and understanding how they are related to one another. Social workers use reflection of feelings to understand how a client responds emotionally to life (Cormier & Cormier, 1991).

The social worker must also be sensitive to nonverbal language, as feelings tend to express themselves nonverbally (i.e., a nervous laugh, a rolling of the eyes, nervous twitching, blushing, or looking down). Additionally, if the client has difficulty expressing a feeling, the social worker may want to present several feeling words, all with similar meanings, so that the client can select the one with the best fit (Kadushin & Kadushin, 1997). This enables the client to confirm the feeling, but without experiencing the pressure of identifying feeling states. The social worker can also normalize feelings (e.g., "Many people who lose a parent feel the way you do—very empty and alone"). Reflection of feeling is a technique that helps the social worker explore the extent of the client's problems and how the client views the problem situation. Validating the client's feelings can be good modeling, showing the client that his or her feelings matter and have a powerful effect on cognition and behavior.

Box 3.1

> **Direct Practice Example.** Eileen is a 35-year-old female attending sessions to help her deal with depression. She has recently remembered episodes of sexual abuse that she experienced as a child by an adult relative. She has managed to avoid the issue for 20 years, but is currently feeling overwhelmed.
>
> Eileen: I just don't know how to deal with this pain.
> Social worker: It's a lot to digest. Right now you're hurting, and feeling very confused.
>   (reflection of feeling)
> Eileen: I just wish I could run away from the world.
> Social worker: Your memories of the abuse are really having an overwhelming effect on you.
>   (reflection of feeling)
> Eileen: I just never really thought about it before. It just makes me so crazy. I'm having a
>   difficult time staying focused at work and at home.
> Social worker: That's understandable. You are trying to make sense of what happened to you. It
>   was a frightening and scary time. (reflection of feeling)
> Eileen: Yeah, it was. I know it is important to deal with this. I've hid it from myself for so many
>   years; I never really let myself *feel* anything.

The social worker in this case is validating Eileen's ambivalent emotions. Eileen begins to realize how the experience of abuse has had a significant impact on her life. By helping Eileen identify the layers of feelings and thoughts, she will gain more insight into her problem, which will lead to progress in functioning more effectively and alleviating feelings of distress. Eileen recognizes that she has hidden her feelings for a long time. By acknowledging this, she has gained insight into how sexual abuse as a child affects her current relationships ("I never really let myself feel anything").

As this example illustrates, it is important for the social worker to have a rich vocabulary of feeling words in order to match the affect of the client, to mirror the client's depth and intensity of feeling. (See the list of feeling words in Appendix B.)

Paraphrasing

This skill focuses on the content of the client's message. The social worker uses paraphrasing to confirm the meaning the client has attached to the messages conveyed throughout the interview. The social worker restates what the client has said, in his or her own words (Hepworth, Rooney & Larsen, 1997). Paraphrasing elicits feedback from the client, confirming that the social worker understands the meaning of the client's message.

Box 3.2

> **Direct Practice Example.** Mary is a 47-year-old female who has been struggling with finances. She spends money excessively and is deeply in debt.
>
> Social worker: What do you experience when you go to the mall? (open-ended question)
> Mary: I go in the evening, especially when I'm feeling stressed. The kids will get me upset and
>   I'll go straight to the mall after dinner.

Box 3.2, con't.

Social worker: Most of the time you go to the mall as a reaction to a difficult situation at home. (paraphrasing)

Mary: Yeah, I'll feel frustrated and then when I go shopping, I get this intense rush. I mean it really works. I charge up my credit cards on a lot of things I really don't need. It gives me a quick thrill. But by the time I get home I feel like crap because I realize that I've just dug myself deeper into debt.

Social worker: Your excessive spending is a way to help you feel better. However, you experience guilt once you get home. (reflection of feeling)

Mary: Yeah, I feel awful and then I feel very worthless. That's when my husband and I fight— and then I just want to get back to the mall. The whole thing just keeps going round and round.

Social worker: So you see this as a pattern or a cycle. You spend money to relieve stress, but then regret your actions. This leads to more stress, and it starts all over. (paraphrasing)

Mary: That's exactly how I see it.

In this example, the social worker captures the true meaning of Mary's addictive spending pattern. Hearing this "cycle" repeated back to her highlights for Mary the major counseling issue: developing other ways to reduce stress and conflict in her life.

Paraphrasing should not be used excessively, so as to avoid conveying the impression that the social worker is simply mimicking what the client is saying (Hepworth, Rooney & Larsen, 1997). It should be used in conjunction with other methods of facilitating the client's responses, such as reflection of feelings and interpretation. Paraphrasing helps the client to see clearly what he or she is thinking or experiencing. Hearing the social worker restate ideas gives the client an opportunity to rethink or to see issues from a different perspective (Hepworth, Rooney & Larsen, 1997).

Open-Ended Questions

Asking questions comes naturally to the social worker. However, asking relevant, purposeful, and insightful questions requires skill. By using an open-ended question such as "Please tell me, what is it like for you at school?" the social worker can prompt the client to elaborate on a point. This gives the client the opportunity to discuss important aspects of the problem in more depth (Kadushin & Kadushin, 1997).

Open-ended questions tend to be general (e.g., "How are you feeling today?"). Once the social worker has an overview of the situation, asking more specific questions will fill in the picture (e.g., "You said that you are very upset about having to talk to me. Please tell me, what aspects of being here trouble you the most?")

When asking an open-ended question, there are two issues to consider: Is the question relevant, and does it help achieve the purpose of the interview? Questions should be phrased in a way that invites a response, not in a way that demands a response (e.g., "Please tell me," versus "I must know"). Questions can take the form of who, what, why, where, when, and how. Open-ended questions tend to begin with "what" ("What happened then?"); "how" ("How did your wife's reaction influence your choice to start drinking again?"); "or "why" ("Why is this so important to you?").

Social workers must be careful, however, in using "why" questions. Frequently, clients don't know why they do something a certain way. Asking them to explain themselves may cause them to become defensive and close down communication. Therefore, "why" questions should be asked with discretion (Sheafor, Horejsi & Horejsi, 1997). If the client becomes angry, use a paraphrase or reflection of feeling response, and then ask the question another way (i.e., instead of "Why are you so sure you can't do it on your own?" ask "Please tell me, what makes being on your own so hard?").

Box 3.3

Direct Practice Example. Latisha is a 30-year-old female client who is struggling with her role as a stepparent. She and her husband Frank are separated; they are attending counseling sessions under court order as part of the divorce decree

Latisha: I never expected that I would have such a hard time parenting a five year old and an eight year old.
Social worker: Latisha, I'd like to know--how do you see your role as a stepmother? (open-ended question)

In this example the question focuses the interview, while still allowing the client to respond in any way she chooses.

If the client responds to an open-ended question with a "yes" or a "no," the social worker can try rephrasing the question. If, after several attempts have failed, change the topic of conversation (e.g., "I can tell that you don't want to talk about Andre. Let's spend some time discussing your housing situation. I know the landlord has decided to refurbish the building. How does this affect you?").

Closed-Ended Questions

A closed-ended question (e.g., "How many times has your daughter run away?") enables the social worker to check details of the client's narrative for accuracy. They also can help gather small, but useful, pieces of information such as date of birth, number of siblings, and number of previous arrests (Cormier & Cormier, 1991).

Closed-ended questions can also bring into focus a particular issue—depending on the answer, the social worker can then follow up with related questions.

Box 3.4

Direct Practice Example. Mario is a 14-year-old male student who has been referred to the social worker due to severe conflicts at home. His parents are threatening to send him to his aunt's home in another city.

Box 3.4, con't.

> Social worker: Tell me about things at home between you and your parents. (open-ended question)
>
> Mario: It's okay. I don't really want to talk about this with you.
>
> Social worker: I know, it's hard to talk to a stranger about your family. (paraphrasing)
>
> Mario: It's not me, it's my parents. They order me around all the time. I can't stand all the yelling.
>
> Social worker: How often do you get yelled at? (closed-ended question)
>
> Mario: Too often, probably 15 times a day.
>
> Social worker: What seems to start the arguments? (open-ended question)

In this example, Mario is initially reluctant to talk. Because the social worker has conveyed her understanding of his situation, he starts communicating. By answering the simple closed-ended question, the client has given the social worker an opening to pursue a deeper understanding of his conflicts with his parents.

Beginning social workers can overuse closed-ended questions. While closed-ended questions are very useful in pinpointing the details of a situation, asking too many in close succession can make for a superficial interview that fails to get at underlying issues (Hepworth, Rooney & Larsen, 1997).

Clarification

This is a skill that allows the social worker to identify what a client is thinking, feeling, and experiencing. When the client's messages are too abstract or hazy, a social worker may ask for the client to be more specific about the meaning of words, or the frequency and duration of problems. Clients may assume that a social worker understands the meaning of their messages and therefore may not fully explain their meaning unless a social worker asks for clarification. For example, an adolescent gang member may state that he "hangs out" with his buddies. The social worker may want to clarify what, precisely, "hanging out" constitutes by asking for details. A client may use qualifiers such as "always," "sometimes," or "kinda." It is important to determine exactly what these qualifiers mean (Cormier & Cormier, 1991).

Clarification should be used when a client is discussing a situation that the social worker does not fully understand. In turn, the social worker must make responses as clear as possible, so the client understands the true meaning of the social worker's words. Clarification thus becomes a reciprocal process between the social worker and the client (Hepworth, Rooney & Larsen, 1997). The social worker may misinterpret the client's messages and develop incorrect perceptions of the client's situation. Therefore, it is essential that the social worker clarify when she or he is uncertain about the client's message, asking, for example, "Is this what you mean?" or "Is this what you're saying?" Additionally, the social worker may want the client to elaborate on a particular topic or to give specific examples regarding the situation, behavior, or feeling (Cormier & Cormier, 1991). Box 3.5 provides an example of the social worker using clarification to better understand the client's point of view.

Box 3.5

Direct Practice Example. Ralph is a 16-year-old male attending sessions with a social worker because of his repeated fighting with other students. He has a long history of behavioral disruptions at school and is in danger of being expelled.

Ralph: It's not fair, the teachers are always busting me for fighting. They have it in for me.
Social worker: You think that 's the reason you're here, because of all the fighting?
    (clarification)
Ralph: Yeah, I was sent to your office because the teachers are definitely out to get me.
Social worker: When you say the teachers are out to get you, what does that mean, exactly?
    (clarification)

In this example the social worker attempts to gain an understanding of Ralph's point of view on his troubles at school. The social worker wants to be certain that they are "speaking the same language" (e.g., "What does that mean, exactly?"). If Ralph is given the opportunity to present and clarify his position without feeling blamed or accused, he is likely to contribute more to the session.

Summarization

When using this skill, the social worker pulls together relevant subjects into a composite response. Both the feeling(s) and content of the client's message are incorporated in the social worker's statement. Summarization is used throughout the therapeutic interview, to focus the discussion on relevant issues as well as to make transitions from one subject to another. Summarizations are also used at the beginning or end of sessions. Generally, a good way to begin a session is to summarize what was discussed in the last session. This technique ensures continuity across sessions. Summarization can also be useful at the end of a session to highlight relevant and related topics, and to set the agenda for the next visit (Hepworth, Rooney & Larsen, 1997.

Box 3.6

Direct Practice Example. Kate is an 18-year-old female who has been living with a foster family since she was eight years old. She is discussing recent events in her life with her social worker, focusing particularly on her relationship with her biological mother.

Kate: Marvin and Julia [foster parents] have taken good care of me. I know that they are proud of
        my accomplishments, especially me getting accepted at the university.
Social worker: You've done so well. You've proven that you can make it. (paraphrasing)
Kate: Yeah! I want to make something of myself. I want to do better than my Mom did for me.
        You know, she didn't even show up for my graduation. Marvin and Julia were there,
        cheering me on.
Social worker: You sound very hurt and disappointed that your Mom didn't come and celebrate
        your special day. (reflection of feeling)
Kate: I know I should have prepared myself—she's not going to show, but I always hope she
        will.

Box 3.6, con't.

Social worker: You're really angry at her right now. (reflection of feeling) Can you tell me more
   about your relationship with her? (open-ended question)
Kate: I don't know. I wish that she wanted to be a part of my life. Sometimes I think she's
   jealous of Marvin and Julia. Maybe she feels bad about everything that has happened,
   especially the stuff with her husband. He never wanted me around and maybe that's part
   of why she stays away too.
Social worker: You love Marvin and Julia, but wish things had turned out differently with your
   Mom. You understand her circumstances, but it doesn't change the fact that you feel hurt
   and let down by her time after time. (summarization)

In this example, Kate talks about several important issues: 1) her relationship with her foster
parents; 2) graduating from high school and going to college; 3) disappointment with her mother,
yet understanding her situation; and 4) wanting to do things differently in her own life. The
social worker pulls together several issues presented by Kate and develops a concise statement
summarizing the important points.

In conclusion, summarization provides focus throughout the interview, highlighting important
points and bringing together themes, patterns, and insights. A summarization is not merely a
"list"; rather, it is a composite of the most significant parts of the interview.

Information Giving

The social worker uses this skill when giving the client useful information. Information may
include available resources in the community such as a local food pantry or a homeless shelter
(Murphy & Dillon, 1998). Or, it might be factual information relevant to the client's presenting
problem (e.g., informing a client with a substance abuse problem about the progressive nature of
an addiction).

Box 3.7

Direct Practice Example. Mandy is a 19-year-old female, who discloses in the middle of a
session that she is very anxious. She recently attended a party where she had unprotected sex
with a man she only knows casually.

Mandy: I can't believe I did this. I mean, it was really stupid.
Social worker: Having unprotected sex could have serious consequences, one of which is getting
   infected with a sexually transmitted disease. (information giving)
Mandy: You mean like AIDS?
Social Worker: Yes. (information giving)
Mandy: But I feel OK
Social worker: The only way you'll know whether you're infected will be to get an HIV antibody
   test in three to six months. (information giving) I know you must be scared about all this.
   (reflection of feeling) Let's talk about what happened last night. (open-ended question)

In this example, Mandy is expressing some concern about her health status, as well as her lack of good judgment in having unprotected sex. The social worker provides relevant information to Mandy and then refocuses the interview on her emotional state.

Social workers present information to educate clients about options, not to dictate those choices in a judgmental way. Keeping within the social work ethic of self-determination, information should always presented in a way that allows the client to accept or reject the information. Specifically, it is important to distinguish between advice and information. Giving "advice" is telling clients what you believe to be in their best interest; providing information allows clients to make choices based on all the available alternatives (Sheafor, Horejsi & Horejsi, 1997).

Finally, if the social worker doesn't have the necessary information, he or she should be honest and amenable to gathering the information for the next session. Providing a reading list, a brochure, or pamphlet about a service or agency can be very empowering to the client.

Interpretation

Interpretation is a skill that the social worker employs to go beyond the client's stated problem and begin to find a deeper meaning. This is a process of getting to underlying issues associated with the problem. Interpretation is helpful because it gets under the surface of the problem as envisioned by the client (Cormier & Cormier, 1991).

Interpretation provides an alternative way of looking at a problem. Frequently, clients are emotionally attached to a problem, and their judgment is clouded. They have difficulty seeing a way out of the situation. Interpretation allows clients to see the problem in a new light, which can give them hope that change is indeed possible.

Box 3.8

Direct Practice Example. José is a 45-year-old male who is experiencing multiple problems. Today he is discussing his boss. This is his third session with the social worker.

José: I hate this guy. He's always looking over my shoulder on the assembly line. So what I do is show up late, I take a few minutes more for lunch. That really gets to him.
Social worker: You do things that you know will irritate your boss. (paraphrasing)
José: Yeah, I mean he never has a kind word to say, he's never given me a raise.
Social worker: Perhaps what you really want is recognition and a sense of being valued on the job. It is an important part of your work ethic and identity. (interpretation)
José: Yeah, you're right. I hadn't really thought about it that way before.

José reports that he purposefully behaves in ways that make his boss angry. The social worker focuses on the underlying issue—not feeling recognized and valued as an employee and as a person. This new insight can help Jose address his own responsibility and hopefully bring about change in his work situation.

Offering an interpretation is a delicate process. The social worker offers a tentative statement and then gauges the client's reaction to find out whether the interpretation was helpful (Cormier & Cormier, 1991). It is important to note that the client may accept or reject the social worker's interpretation. The client may offer his or her own interpretation if the one offered by the social worker doesn't fit. Success in using this skill is very dependent on the length, timing, and quality of the social worker–client relationship. Interpretation is most beneficial when the social worker and the client have a good rapport, and the client appears ready to explore underlying issues related to the problem (Kadushin & Kadushin, 1997).

As the social worker offers an interpretation, he or she should be alert to the client's verbal and **nonverbal responses**. Interpretation can stimulate a variety of feelings in the client. If the social worker feels that the client needs additional support to deal with the new insight, then interpretation should be paired with reflection of feeling or paraphrasing (Hepworth, Rooney & Larsen, 1997).

Confrontation

This is a skill that a social worker uses to address a discrepancy in the client's message (Hepworth, Rooney & Larsen, 1997). This discrepancy can take two forms: behavior versus statement or statement versus statement. Sometimes, a discrepancy exists between two or more of the client's messages. The client may deny that she is experiencing stress in her relationship with her husband; however, within the same session she reports that she hates talking to him. The social worker points out this discrepancy.

It may be difficult for the client to accept or acknowledge identified discrepancies. Therefore, it is important that the social worker has developed a strong therapeutic relationship with the client before confronting any discrepancies. For confrontation to be used effectively in the helping relationship, the social worker must first establish a trusting and safe environment with the client. This will lower the client's defensiveness and reduce the client's anxiety and feelings of being "attacked." Confrontation is a skill that should be used sparingly, and with a great deal of support from the social worker. This skill helps clients address issues that they may have been avoiding. A confrontation is also helpful in identifying the reality of the situation, versus the client's distortion (Hepworth, Rooney & Larsen, 1997).

Box 3.9

Direct Practice Example. Elaine is a 45-year-old married female who is the mother of three teenage sons. Recently, her 75-year-old father, who has been diagnosed with Alzheimer's disease, has come to live with the family following his wife's death.

Elaine: Dad can be so demanding of my time and energy. I know this is related to the Alzheimer's, but…
Social worker: You can end up feeling very overwhelmed. (reflection of feeling)
Elaine: Yeah, especially when I get so little help from my husband and kids. They all head off to their activities, leaving me alone with Dad. Then Dad starts to wander out of the house while I'm getting dinner ready. I can't just let him wander off, so I have to lock him in his room.
Social worker: I hear the frustration you're experiencing. (reflection of feeling) However, locking your father in his room is not okay. It's illegal, and it could be very dangerous. (confrontation)

Box 3.9, con't.

Elaine: I know you're right, but I don't know any other way to keep him safe.

Social worker: I understand the dilemma—caring for your dad, your husband, and your children leaves you feeling exhausted and depleted. (summarization)

In this example, the social worker confronts Elaine about the treatment of her father. She points out the problems related to leaving him locked him in his room. She also conveys understanding of the frustrations associated with caring an elderly parent. Because Elaine feels understood, she is more likely to acknowledge the dangers involved in her choice. The next step in the helping process will involve discussions between the social worker and Elaine on how to improve her father's care and maintain a balance in her life.

It is essential that the social worker use confrontation after a therapeutic relationship has been established (Egan, 1997). A confrontation that occurs too early in a therapeutic relationship or when the client doesn't feel comfortable with the social worker could have a detrimental effect. The client is likely to become defensive and angry. Confrontation should be used sparingly, with professional discretion, and always with the best interest of the client in mind.

Attending Behaviors

Social workers must be verbally and nonverbally responsive to clients. One way that a social worker conveys interest is through the use of words; another way is through nonverbal communication. It is important for the client to feel listened to and valued. If clients sense a genuine interest on the social worker's part, they will be more open (Kadushin & Kadushin, 1997). The social presence, being fully there and available, is instrumental in the establishment and further development of the relationship.

There are several ways that the social worker can communicate concern, caring, and involvement with the client nonverbally. Tone of voice, eye contact, body positioning, head movements, furthering responses, and mirroring the client's emotional/facial responses are all components of this skill, known as attending behavior (Cormier & Cormier, 1991). Body positioning, what we communicate through hand gestures, leaning in and facing our clients, and maintaining a relaxed and approachable stance are all important ways of conveying "I'm here with you, you have my undivided attention."

Seating arrangements will be dependent on the setting of the interview. If visiting a client's home, wait for the client to indicate where to sit. In an office, it is best to place the chairs about three to four feet apart. This distance appears to be the least anxiety provoking for the client (Cormier & Cormier, 1991). Always be aware of the client's need for personal space and be respectful of this need by allowing the client to determine the most comfortable distance. Should three to four feet not be enough or too much, allow the client to adjust accordingly. This is of particular concern when working with clients from different cultural backgrounds. If the client pulls the chair too close, invading your personal space, either subtly move back your chair or tactfully ask the client to move back a bit.

Touch is also a part of how a social worker uses his or her body to convey interest. Touch can be perceived as positive or negative, depending on the type of touch and the context in which it occurs (Cormier & Cormier, 1991). Always be aware of the client's cultural background and past experiences, such as having been sexually abused as a child), and gender-related issues (i.e., could the touch be interpreted by the client as a sexual overture?). Used correctly, touch can be a very potent, nonverbal way of communicating "I care, I'm listening, and I'm concerned." A nonthreatening way to attend to a client who is crying is to offer a tissue, attending to the need without actual touch.

Maintaining eye contact with the client conveys understanding and responsiveness (Kadushin & Kadushin, 1997). This is not the same as staring or glaring at a client, which can cause extreme discomfort. Eye contact on the part of the client and/or social worker can demonstrate a readiness to get down to "business" and delve into the problem situation.

Tone of voice, whether the client's or the social worker's, is another aspect of attending behavior. It is not just the spoken words, but the way the words are delivered (Cormier & Cormier, 1991). Tone of voice adds color and richness to the message. As an example:

Box 3.10

Social worker: You sound really sad (said in a quiet, soft tone).
Client: I am very depressed, I've never felt worse I my life.
Social worker: It makes sense, you are still in mourning over your son's death (said with an intonation of sadness).

Here the social worker matches the tone of voice to the words chosen. The client thus experiences the social worker's concern at many levels.

Furthering responses offered by the social worker are another way of conveying understanding. Furthering responses can be used to highlight a particular word (e.g., Client: I doubt he'll ever forgive me! Social worker: Forgive you?). Hand gestures or nodding of the head are other ways of nonverbally communicating that the social worker is listening and for the client to continue.

Single word utterances, such as "hmmm," "uh-huh," and "um" also convey an interest in the client and serve as inducements for the client to proceed, as the following example illustrates.

Box 3.11

Client: My daughter refuses to discuss her finances with me, but she insists she has no money and needs a loan.
Social worker: A loan?
Client: A loan, for something, but she won't tell me what. That leaves me thinking the worst, like she owes money to a loan shark.
Social worker: And…
Client: It scares me to death. I don't want anyone coming after her or me.
Social worker: That is unsettling. (paraphrasing) Do you have any other ideas about what's going on with her? (open-ended question)
Client: No, but she always ends up in some kind of trouble, with me bailing her out.

Box 3.11, con't.

Social worker: uh hmmm.
Client: I know she counts on me to help her and I usually do, but I won't lend her money unless she tells me what it is for.

Social worker: That makes a lot of sense. (information giving)

Through a reflection of feeling statement, social workers convey to clients an understanding of their experiences. Social workers can also do this nonverbally by using facial expressions to mirror back to the client awareness of the client's emotional state.

It is also imperative for the social worker to attend to the interplay of the client's words and facial expressions (e.g., "I feel great" as the client grins from ear to ear, versus "I feel great" as tears stream down the client's face). Using this example, the social worker can respond to "the tears versus the words" by saying "Although you say you feel great, your tears tell me something different. I'd like to talk about the sadness you're experiencing right now."

The social worker's facial expressions should reinforce the verbal communication (i.e., saying I'm interested in hearing your side of the story and looking interested in the client, not looking bored or distracted). This nonverbal display of interest can speak volumes to the client and serve as a reinforcement to continue.

The social worker's head movements can also offer nonverbal feedback to the client as a way of encouraging or discouraging the client from further discussion. Head nodding up and down offers a sense that the social worker is listening and agreeing. Because the client feels understood, the communication is likely to continue. Shaking of the head from left to right may convey that the social worker disagrees or disapproves, causing the communication to stop or be severely limited.

INTEGRATING SOCIAL WORK SKILLS AND ATTENDING BEHAVIOR

Each skill is presented in this chapter as a discrete element. However, the skills work best when used in combination with one another. The social work interview becomes richer and deeper in meaning when skills are used in tandem. The following example pairs an open-ended question with a paraphrase:

Box 3.12

Social worker: You said the days just drag on and on as you wait for a phone call about your daughter. (paraphrase) How do you manage to get through the day? (open-ended question)
Client: I try to keep myself busy. Since she ran away I haven't really been able to sleep much. I wake up because I have these dreadful nightmares. My husband seems to be handling this better than I am. He almost acts as if none of this is happening.

Box 3.12, con't.

Social worker: That must make it seem even more difficult for you, almost like you're in this alone. (paraphrase; the social worker leans toward the client, maintaining eye contact) What is your relationship with him like right now? (open-ended question)

In the next example the social worker uses reflection of feeling, information giving, and a closed-ended question.

Box 3.13

Client: I don't know whether I'm doing the right thing leaving my husband. We don't have any place to stay.
Social worker: Um hmm. (furthering response) Right now you are struggling to find a place to live, and you're worried about what will happen to your children. (reflection of feeling) There are some temporary shelters in our community that offer a safe place to stay. (information giving) Would you like the phone number for one? (closed-ended question)

CONCLUSION

When social work skills are first used by the beginning social worker, they can seem mechanical. With time and practice, they will become almost second nature. Keep in mind, though, that even the most experienced social workers benefit from an ongoing commitment to improve their interview skills. Through contact with other social workers, membership in professional organizations such as NASW, and most importantly, the development of the habit of self-evaluation, attention to social work skills is a career-long pursuit for social workers.

FOR FURTHER READING

Cormier, W. & Cormier, S. (1991). *Interviewing strategies for helpers*, 3rd ed. Pacific Grove, CA: Brooks/Cole.

DeJong, P. & Miller, S. (1995). How to interview for client strengths. *Social Work Journal 40*(6), 729-736.

Egan, G. (1997). *The skilled helper*, 6th ed. Pacific Grove, CA: Brooks/Cole.

Hepworth, D., Rooney, R., & Larsen, J. (1997). *Direct Social Work Practice: Theory and skills*, 5th ed. Pacific Grove, CA: Brooks/Cole.

Kadushin, A. & Kadushin, G. (1997). *The social work interview*, 4th ed. New York: Columbia University Press.

Sheafor, B., Horejsi, C. & Horejsi, G. (1997). *Techniques and guidelines for social work practice*, 4th ed. Boston, MA: Allyn & Bacon.

Chapter 4
Pitfalls

DETECTING MISTAKES

Knowing how and when to correctly use social work interviewing skills provides the foundation for the helping relationship. Developing the competence to utilize the skills is a learned process. Skills are not used in isolation but in conjunction with each other as a way to further deepen and expand the relationship. Social workers strive to ask the "perfect" open-ended question, or deliver the "perfect" paraphrase, but even the most skilled professionals make mistakes. The goal of this chapter is to provide an explanation of the mistakes, or pitfalls, commonly made by beginning social workers and the negative consequences that may result. Being aware of the pitfalls, "what not to do," can help the social worker avoid potential problems that could damage or abruptly end the social worker–client relationship. When a client reacts (verbally or nonverbally) with embarrassment, anger, or silence, the social worker may have inadvertently fallen into one of the common interviewing pitfalls.

THE PITFALLS

Advice Giving

Social workers should never tell the client what to do to solve the problem; it is vital to the helping process that the client be an active participant. The ethic of self-determination is critical because the purpose of the social work relationship is to empower the client to make decisions that will improve his or her own life (Kadushin & Kadushin, 1997). The client will ultimately live with the consequences of decisions, weighing the costs of each decision that is made.

It is the social worker's role to help clients discover options for probable solutions and together agree on a realistic direction. The social worker helps the client learn about how past decisions have affected life circumstances in positive or negative ways. The client must examine the current situation from a clear perspective. Social workers who are new to the field may have an inclination to give the client advice within the therapeutic relationship, with the potential of establishing an unhealthy dependence (Hepworth, Rooney & Larsen, 1997). Although it is tempting to apply a "quick fix" to a problem situation, if the problem stems from deep-rooted patterns of dysfunctional behavior it will eventually reemerge if the origins of these behaviors are not thoroughly explored.

Box 4.1

> **Pitfall Example.** Steve is a divorced male who has been involved in a string of unhealthy relationships. He asks the social worker about his current relationship, wondering why his girlfriend is so verbally abusive and what he should do to remedy the problem. The practitioner

Box 4.1, con't.

should refrain from giving him prescribed advice. Instead, the social worker should explore the nature of the relationship and the dynamics that are perpetuated not only by the girlfriend but also by Steve.

Inappropriate Use of Humor

When a social worker uses humor inappropriately, the client can feel belittled. The client may believe that you are minimizing the problem and not taking it seriously. Never use sarcasm or humor to make light of the client's problem (Kadushin & Kadushin, 1997). Additionally, sarcasm may be misunderstood by the client, creating a climate of mistrust in the social worker–client relationship. If the social worker makes a humorous comment this could deeply anger the client. The social worker may find humor in the client's situation, but the client may not have the same subjective perspective. Inappropriate humor can also convey that the social worker is not empathic or sensitive to the client's point of view (Kadushin & Kadushin, 1997).

Box 4.2

Pitfall Example. Maurice is a 45-year-old client who is frustrated because he has been unable to find a job. Cracking a joke about being homeless or begging on the streets is ill timed and insensitive. Maurice will assume that you are not taking his unemployment situation seriously and will feel foolish for coming to you in the first place.

The client may use humor to mask a problem. The social worker must be aware of this possibility and search for deeper meaning in the client's message (Hepworth, Rooney & Larsen 1997). Certainly humor has its place in any human relationship, and it can lighten the tension of a situation. In a counseling relationship there may be humorous moments; however, it should never get in the way of the professional helping process. It is very common that the general gravity of what clients discuss in social service settings is quite serious and emotionally charged. Thus humor should be used with great discretion (Kadushin & Kadushin, 1997).

Interrupting the Client/Abrupt Transitions

In the course of an interview, social workers ask many questions. The social worker who is attuned to the client is an active listener and aware of the verbal and nonverbal cues signifying that the client has not finished speaking. Too many interruptions may cause the client to lose his or her train of thought, or to feel that the social worker does not care about the problem. As a consequence, the focus of the interview tends to be more on the social worker than on the client's concerns. Inappropriate interruptions can be annoying and disruptive to the client, and may divert the client from exploring important areas and feelings (Hepworth, Rooney & Larsen, 1997)

Box 4.3

> **Pitfall Example.** Jamie is a 25-year-old drug addict. She begins to give the social worker details related to her drug history and usage. Before she is able to complete her statement, the social worker interrupts Jamie with a question. In this case, the focus shifts from the client to the social worker. Jamie is likely to feel cut off and frustrated. It's possible that Jamie might have revealed important information about her situation, but the opportunity has been lost.

A well-paced interview includes taking turns speaking (Cormier & Cormier, 1991). Both the client and the social worker may need sufficient time to put together what it is they want to say, to ask, how to respond, etc. There may be some silences. However, unfilled space is preferred to cutting the client off. Silence can be an effective tool the social worker uses in helping the client realize what is being discussed (Kadushin & Kadushin, 1997). It also allows the social worker to make nonverbal observations of the client.

Inappropriate and Irrelevant Questions

Be careful not to "overquestion" the client. Asking too many questions may make the interview seem more like an interrogation than a helping session (Egan, 1997). Use questions to get only needed information. While the social worker may be curious about the client's story beyond what is relevant to the interview, only questions that pertain to the helping process should be asked. Irrelevant questions do not produce new and helpful information. Irrelevant questions may also diffuse the importance of the therapeutic relationship, causing the client to feel that the problem solving process is ineffective. Asking questions unrelated to the problem can cause a lack of focus in the session, leading the client to feel distracted and misunderstood.

Box 4.4

> **Pitfall Example.** Ramon is a 14-year-old male who has a long history of school truancy and consequently is failing all of his classes. The social worker begins to ask Ramon a series of questions related to his whereabouts during the school day. Ramon responds with single-word answers and begins to feel accused and interrogated by the social worker. He is likely to retreat even further, perceiving the social worker as hostile, not helpful.

Questions should not be stacked (asking the client two or more questions at a time). These stacked questions may be confusing, leaving the client unsure as to how to respond. This can also diffuse the significance of each question, as the client is considering one question only to be distracted by another (Hepworth, Rooney & Larsen, 1997).

Judgmental Response

The client is coming to the social worker for help, not judgment. Part of the social worker's role is to understand the client's problems. With that understanding the social worker helps the client to find solution(s) to the problem. If the client perceives that he or she is being labeled or judged, a defensive response may occur that will delay or impede the development of trust between the client and the social worker. This could create further difficulties in the helping relationship because the client will not feel comfortable discussing personal information and may view the relationship as an adversarial one (Hepworth, Rooney & Larsen, 1997).

Box 4.5

Pitfall Example. Lisa is a 30-year-old female who has recently "come out" to friends and family about her relationship with Melody, her partner. Today, Lisa discloses that she is exploring the possibility of becoming pregnant through artificial insemination. The social worker responds negatively to her plan, stating, "It's one thing to be a lesbian, it's another to bring a child into this. Have you thought about how your child will be affected by your decision?" Lisa will likely react with disbelief, in part because up to this point the social worker has appeared supportive of her lifestyle. Now that the social worker's true feelings (judgments) have surfaced, Lisa is likely to respond defensively and with anger and therefore withdraw from the helping relationship.

Judgmental responses made by the social worker clearly violate the social work ethic of a nonjudgmental attitude and acceptance (Hepworth, Rooney & Larsen, 1997). Judgmental responses carry with them the social worker's ethical, moral, or political standards. The client may take into account the social worker's judgmental remarks when thinking of his or her own self-concept. Such remarks are detrimental to the entire helping process.

Offering False Assurance

Although a social worker should always look for strength and hope in a client's situation, being realistic and honest is imperative (Hepworth, Rooney & Larsen, 1997). When the social worker provides false assurance, the client's problem is minimized. False assurances can also cause the client to overlook possible roadblocks, thereby making a problem worse. The client must come to terms with the difficulties and possible consequences of the situation. These realizations help prepare the client to take action.

Box 4.6

Pitfall Example. Rose is a 70-year-old resident of a nursing home. She has been there for two weeks and is eagerly waiting to be discharged into her daughter's care. Today, her daughter Eve called, stating, "Mom can't move in with us; my husband refuses to let her stay here, even for a few weeks." The social worker says, "I'm sure that you can convince him to reconsider. Really, your mom is doing much better and I'm certain she would not get in his way at all." The social worker ignores Eve's concerns and jumps directly into offering assurances. Clearly, the social worker wants to gloss over the problems and focus on **her** task--discharge planning. This approach serves the needs of the social worker, not the client. Eve isn't heard or understood, causing her to feel even more confused and guilty.

False assurances may overlook the client's feelings of discomfort, hopelessness, or despair. However, it is also important for the social worker not to be *overly* sympathetic toward the client's situation; the social worker should strive to convey understanding, not pity (Hepworth, Rooney & Larsen, 1997).

Inappropriate Social Worker Self-Disclosure

Although the social worker and client may have much in common, the focus of the session should be on the client's concerns. By sharing too much personal information, the client may assume that you are a friend, not a professional (Murphy & Dillon, 1998).

Box 4.7

> **Pitfall Example.** Daniel is a 50-year-old Jewish scholar who has been in counseling for three months. His presenting problems focus on his relationship with his wife, Marion. The social worker discloses that she converted from Judaism to Catholicism in order to marry her husband. This self-disclosure has the potential to harm the helping relationship. Given Daniel's strong faith and religious background, he may have a difficult time separating his feelings related to her conversion. He now has information that may change his view of the social worker, causing him to be distracted from the problems related to **his** marriage.

Going into details about the social worker's life experience is distracting. The client may feel uncomfortable and put on the spot to respond to the social worker's message (Kadushin & Kadushin, 1997). However, providing general information can help to establish and maintain a relationship (e.g., saying, "I have children, too. They can be a handful," instead of "Let me tell you about my daughter, Susan. She is such a handful. Last night...").

Social worker self-disclosure must be relevant to the client's problem (Kadushin & Kadushin, 1997). Never reveal any information that might be detrimental to the helping process (i.e., "I was arrested for drunk driving 15 years ago").
The social worker needs to be careful not to disclose feeling of disapproval or shock. The client may interpret this as judgment or disbelief. "I'm totally disgusted by what you just told me, how could you hurt your wife like that."

Premature Confrontation

The social worker must approach the client with respect and concern. Challenging the client too early in the relationship can hinder the development of trust and confidence (Kadushin & Kadushin, 1997). At the early stage of the relationship, the client may not believe that the confrontation is in his or her best interest (Egan, 1997). Before confronting a client about inconsistencies between stated goals and behavior, the social worker should be able to answer "yes" to the following question: Have I demonstrated my ability to help the client concerning less volatile issues?

Box 4.8

> **Pitfall Example.** Jacob is a 30-year-old single parent. His wife abandoned the family five months ago, leaving him to care for their sons, ages eight and four. Jacob is currently unemployed and reports that he is looking for a job, but has been unsuccessful in his efforts. The social worker believes that Jacob has a drinking problem and that he was fired because of his sporadic attendance and poor job performance. The social worker confronts him with suspicions,

Box 4.8, con't.

> stating, "I think that you have a problem with alcohol, and that's why your wife left and you are out of a job." Jacob feels attacked by the social worker and refuses to continue in treatment, stating, "How dare you accuse me of having an alcohol problem? I'm out of here."

Overwhelming the Client with Too Much Information

Giving the client too much information makes it difficult to identify what is the most important part of the social worker's message. Excessive information can overwhelm the client and confuse critical issues that the client must take time to consider (Egan, 1997). Presenting information in small doses, from most to least significant, can assist the client in taking necessary action (e.g., "Let's talk about finding a safe place for you tonight. Tomorrow you can contact the State's Attorney about an Order of Protection against your husband.").

Box 4.9

> **Pitfall Example.** Sherry is a 40-year-old stay-at-home mother with three children, ages nine, seven, and five. She has expressed an interest in going back to school and getting an undergraduate degree in education. She has some concerns regarding admission procedures, financial aid requirements, and her ability to do college-level coursework. The social worker states, "There are so many details to getting into the university. First you have to get a copy of your high school transcript to send in with the application. Then you will fill out the application and send a $50.00 check to cover the cost of processing your application. Financial aid and loans are available too, especially because you are a returning student." Because Sherry has been given too much important information at once, it is difficult for her to sort out what her priorities. She is left feeling confused and overwhelmed with details. It is possible that she may not act on her plan because it feels so daunting.

Providing too much information may undermine the client's self-efficacy. Be careful to let the client determine life choices (Murphy & Dillon, 1998). Far from empowering the client with new knowledge, giving too much information may also cause the client to become confused about all of the options. The timing of information is critical. Is the client ready to hear what the social worker is sharing? Preparing the client for emotionally potent information is best done in small doses (Egan,1997).

Premature Problem Solving

Social workers are skilled at problem solving. This does not mean solving the problem for the client. A full understanding of the problem is necessary in order to help the client choose the next step (Hepworth, Rooney & Larsen, 1997). The client typically explores the problem from a process of exploring and evolving understanding. What may be the apparent problem may be a symptom of another layer of dysfunction or the result of associated patterns of behavior.

Box 4.10

Pitfall Example. David is a 40-year-old homeless veteran. He has been living in shelters off and on for the past four years. He is eligible, but is not receiving benefits from the Veterans Administration and Social Security. David has come to the shelter for the night. He informs the social worker that he is a veteran and hasn't received a check for one year. He appears somewhat disheveled and disoriented during the intake interview. The social worker says, "The first thing we have to do is get your benefits reinstated." The social worker completely overlooks his current situation and begins to focus on financial resources. Although this is a viable avenue to explore with David, his immediate need of food and shelter was completely ignored.

Remember, what the client presents as "the problem" this may not be the "real problem." Therefore, if the social worker jumps to problem solving, the social worker may miss essential information that could help resolve the problem.

Insincerity/Lack of Genuineness

Coming across to a client as being artificial or insincere can cause the client to become suspicious of the social worker's intentions. A straightforward and honest manner communicates authenticity (Sheafor, Horejsi & Horejsi, 1997; Kadushin & Kadushin, 1997). Clients can detect a social worker pretending to care, or to listen, very easily. Simply going through the motions, responding with little interest or concern, detracts from the helping relationship.

Box 4.11

Pitfall Example. Irving is an 80-year-old male, currently a patient in a rehabilitation hospital. He suffered from a stroke last month and his recovery process has been slow and painful. He wants to regain all of his capacities, and he is currently expressing frustration at himself and others. Having heard this at every session, the social worker uses a very harsh and angry tone of voice to say, "Irving, you will get better, just be patient." Although the words are reassuring, the tone of the social worker's voice conveys a lack of care or concern. Irving is likely to feel even more frustrated and isolated by his circumstances and withdraw from the relationship.

Minimizing the Problem

For the client to feel understood, the social worker must be able to communicate a full understanding of the significance of the situation (Cormier & Cormier, 1991). The client may be feeling overwhelmed by circumstances—to offer support, the social worker should use words that capture the intensity of the problem. If the social worker misses the intensity (e.g., Client: I am so angry I could just strangle him. Social Worker: You sound sort of upset right now.), the client may wonder whether the social worker truly understands.

Box 4.12

Pitfall Example. Theresa is a 12-year-old 7th grader. Her parents recently informed her that because of her mother's job change, they will be moving to a new community. Theresa doesn't want to leave her friends and school. She is afraid of moving, in part because it has always been

Box 4.12, con't.

difficult for her to make friends. She is very shy and introverted. The social worker says, "Moving can be fun and exciting, and you'll be able to start off with a clean slate." Although the social worker's response may be true, Theresa's concerns are not addressed. The social worker attempts to reduce the complexity of the issue to a single statement. Theresa is likely to feel unheard, causing her to retreat even further.

If the client senses an implicit message of "it's no big deal, why are you bothering me" from the social worker, the client is likely to withdraw from the relationship. The client may also feel that he or she is overreacting, based on the social worker's minimal reaction.

Remember that the client may also attempt to minimize the impact of the problem situation. The social worker uses problem identification and assessment skills to analyze underlying issues (perhaps unexpressed or downplayed by the client) that determine the severity of the problem.

LEARNING FROM MISTAKES

When mistakes are made during an interview, the social worker's goal should be to learn from the experience, so that when presented with a similar situation, he or she can respond with a new level of professionalism. Sometimes, social workers fail to recognize pitfalls. However, clients often react in ways that highlight mistakes (e.g., "That's not what I said," or nonverbal cues such as avoiding eye contact) when the social worker has said something that has hurt, angered, or offended them.

A social worker who has just responded to a client in a judgmental manner should apologize and start over ("I can tell my comment has made you very upset. I'm sorry, that was not my intent. Let me rephrase what I was trying to say"). This is a face-saving measure for both the social worker and the client. Hopefully, the relationship has not been permanently affected, and the client and the social worker can move on in the problem-solving process. Through practicing the social work skills and maintaining an awareness of common pitfalls, social workers can achieve a positive, helping relationship with clients.

FOR FURTHER READING

Dorner, D. (1996). *The logic of failure: Why things go wrong and what we can do to make them right*. New York: Holt.

Herlihy, B. & Corey, G. (1997). *Boundary issues in counseling: Multiple roles and responsibilities*. Alexandria, VA: American Counseling Association.

Kottler, J.A. (Ed.) (1997). *Finding your way as a counselor*. Alexandria, VA: American Counseling Association.

Kottler, J.A. & Blau, D.S. (1989). *The imperfect therapist: Learning from failure in therapeutic practice*. San Francisco, CA: Jossey-Bass.

Lee, C.C. & Richardson, B.L. (1991). Problems and pitfalls of multicultural counseling. In C.C. Lee & B.L. Richardson (Eds.), *Multicultural issues in counseling: New approaches to diversity* (pp. 3–9). Alexandria, VA: American Association for Counseling and Development.

Chapter 5
Cultural Diversity

The rapidly changing cultural demographics of the United States have led experts to predict that minorities will dominate the population in the near future (Ashford, Lecroy, & Lortie, 1997; Murphy & Dillon, 1998; Comas-Diaz & Greene, 1994). Increasingly, social workers can expect to work with individuals and families from diverse cultural backgrounds. Social workers have an ethical responsibility to be culturally competent (National Association of Social Workers [NASW], 1997). This means that social workers need to acquire knowledge of a variety of cultural dimensions such as attitudes, values, customs, communication patterns, gender roles, and spirituality that define particular cultures (Murphy & Dillon, 1998). Culturally competent social workers engage clients within the boundaries of their culture, and therefore, must structure agency delivery systems in ways that are flexible enough to respond effectively to the needs of diverse populations. (NASW, 1997).

Acquiring cultural sensitivity is an ongoing process that requires a commitment from the social worker to become culturally competent. Acting on that commitment, social workers involve themselves in professional training on multiculturalism, seeking out social experiences with different cultural groups, and being willing to become a student of culturally diverse client groups. While growing in knowledge and competence in the area of multiculturalism, it is important for the social worker not to construct a fixed conception about any particular ethnic group (Zastrow & Kirst-Ashman, 1997). Many stereotypes have been constructed and perpetrated on individuals and groups of minority status in the name of being "culturally sensitive." While different cultures can be understood in the context of specific values, beliefs and customs, to automatically apply this cultural knowledge to every member of a the group denies the uniqueness of every individual (Ashford, Lecroy, & Lortie, 1997; Queralt, 1996). Many factors, such as immigration and demographic patterns, acculturation, assimilation, socioeconomic status, and educational background can cause significant differences within a particular group. All individuals possess an array of characteristics that fall within and outside of their proclaimed cultural identity. Some characteristics may reflect a particular "cultural norm" while other behaviors may run counter to your expectations (Zastrow & Kirst-Ashman, 1997). For instance, a Mexican family living in Los Angeles will have a different experience and access to resources than will a Mexican migrant family living in southwest Texas.

Cultural identity is defined here as the extent to which an individual identifies with and relates to a particular group. In reality, cultural identity runs along a continuum from absolute singular identification, to an association with two or more cultural groups (McGoldrick, Giordano, & Pearce, 1996). Where someone falls on the continuum is influenced by agents of socialization, geographic location (i.e., rural versus urban), socioeconomic status, race, religion, politics, and migration patterns. The intensity of one's cultural connection may impede one's opportunities. In mainstream U.S. society, when the values and customs of one group run counter to mainstream beliefs and practices, group members may find many doors closed to them in employment, political, and education arenas, unless the individual chooses acculturation as an adaptive mode. For example, an Orthodox Jewish male may not progress up the corporate ladder as fast as his non-Jewish colleagues because of his strict adherence to religious practices, such as keeping the Sabbath, maintaining a kosher lifestyle, and wearing traditional Orthodox dress. Acculturation is an adaptive process for fitting into a culture different from one's own. Acculturation occurs when one learns the norms and customs of a culture other than one's own, without giving up one's cultural identity. When people begin to move beyond the boundaries of their own culture into another culture in order to adapt and survive, they may experience a cultural clash (Lee, 1996; and Queralt, 1996). For example, when an Appalachian woman violates cultural norms of subservience and domestic responsibilities, and makes the decision to enter law school, she may find herself in inner conflict between following one's aspirations (becoming a lawyer) and adhering to her family and community's cultural gender norms (being subservient and domestic). In a sense, acculturation is akin to navigating one's life with one foot in two different worlds. Some refer to this living in two worlds simultaneously as biculturation (DeAndre, 1984; Queralt, 1996).

When assimilation occurs, a person of a diverse culture is immersed in another culture, shedding his or her original cultural identity (Queralt, 1996). The classic example of assimilation is when first generation immigrants desire to parent their children within the norms of the mainstream culture, and de-emphasize their culture of origin. For example, a Mexican family immigrating to the United States may teach their children English, and not speak Spanish in their home. While some immigrants may attempt assimilation and the total adoption of the norms of their new home, total assimilation may not occur, since it requires acceptance of the members of that society (Atkinson, Morten, & Sue 1998).

The level of acculturation and assimilation must be taken into account when providing services to client systems. The social worker should avoid making presumptions about the client's cultural identity. Individuals are often influenced by more than one culture and personify this in their daily lives. For example, a gay Brazilian male may live openly with his partner, thus defying the Brazilian rigid gender roles and heterosexual expectations of that culture. At the same time, he adheres to the cultural norms of close family ties by attending all family functions and visiting his mother weekly and providing her with financial assistance.

The pursuit of cultural sensitivity is an *ongoing process* of learning of cultural differences, and implementing professional interventions that will help rather than hinder a client's growth. Social workers make interpretations of clients' actions and words that reflect their personal cultural roots. To effectively engage a client from a diverse culture, social workers need to move beyond their own cultural norms and beliefs and enter into the client's cultural stream. In doing so, the social worker is able to ascertain the client's world view, and structure interventions that are culturally appropriate and helpful. For example, the diagnosis of major depression, as defined in the Diagnostic and Statistical Manual of Mental Disorders IV (DSM IV) include some of the following: 1) inability to experience pleasure in daily activities; 2) feelings of worthlessness; 3) inappropriate guilt; and 4) recurring thoughts of death (American Psychiatric Association, 1994). These criteria emerged from a Western worldview. In traditional Mexican culture, people often describe their problems from a paradoxical and fatalistic perspective. It is culturally appropriate to give a passionate description of one's life difficulties. When seeing a social worker, a traditional Mexican woman may express her current concerns in the following way: "This job is killing me." "I'm in a dark ditch and no one wants to help me." "I have a lot of luck, a lot of bad luck." "Jesus Christ carried his cross for a day, I've carried mine for 50 years." The traditional American social worker would most likely view the client as having little self worth and a bleak outlook on life, and possibly consider the client as depressed. The culturally competent social worker would recognize that fatalistic language is common among traditional Mexicans, and that the client may be expressing that she has endured hardships, and is therefore strong, self-reliant, and capable of dealing with life's circumstances (Madrigal, 1995). The ethically responsible social worker recognizes that being culturally competent is an essential component of effective social work practice.

Social work skills such as empathic responses, genuineness, and clarification are helpful in establishing therapeutic relationships across all cultural lines. However, the social worker committed to cultural competence moves beyond the basic skills of social work and seeks methods of engaging diverse populations in specific, accurate, and effective ways of problem solving. Building a culturally sensitive practice is an ongoing process; one never "arrives." Box 5.1 provides a set of guidelines for social workers to follow in developing a culturally sensitive practice.

Box 5.1

Guidelines for developing a culturally sensitive practice
1. Examine how your own cultural values and practices color your interpretation of client events;
2. Be open to experiencing and learning about other cultures;
3. Recognize strengths within different cultures;
4. Assess the client's level of comfort in the clinical arena, and maximize your efforts to put the client at ease through the use of cultural knowledge;
5. Be aware of institutional barriers that may prevent clients from diverse cultures from accessing services and resources;
6. Be aware of verbal and nonverbal messages within different cultural contexts;
7. Be amenable to soliciting information about various cultures from a number of sources, such as involvement in culturally diverse groups, attending conferences on multiculturalism, and being open to learn from the client;
8. Learn more about the historical background of the cultures that you serve, including traditions, values, practices;
9. Be aware of social and community resources to which the client can be referred;
10. Adapt agency delivery systems to fit within the culture that you serve;

Box 5.1, con't.

11. Have interpreters available and seek to hire social workers who are fluent in the language of your major client groups; and
12. Be able to distinguish the difference between cultural characteristics and real dysfunction.

(Kadushin & Kadushin, 1997; McGoldrick, Giordano, & Pearce, 1996; and Sheafor, Horejsi, & Horejsi, 1997)

Through the assessment process, the social worker should identify the influences of culture(s) on the client (Queralt, 1996). Culture has a strong impact on how people perceive issues, the degree to which they are willing to discuss feelings and personal problems, and how they approach problem solving. For example, a social worker who is working with a Haitian family realizes they are inactive and nonverbal in the initial sessions. Through cultural training, the social worker learns that many Haitians disapprove of therapy because of their belief that God will take care of every aspect of their lives. Instead of confronting the clients' inactivity, the social worker takes time to learn from the clients about their beliefs and how these beliefs play an important role in their lives (Bibb and Casimir, 1996).

In a multitude of ways, culture influences how one views one's self and others. Although culture plays an important part in people's thoughts and behaviors, there are individual differences within every culture. Many clients live biculturally, selectively adopting parts of their culture of origin and mainstream American culture. For example, Lourdes is a 17-year-old Peruvian American who is failing her courses because of a recent breakup with her boyfriend. She has been referred to the school social worker. Lourdes also has a volatile relationship with her father, a traditional Peruvian who has difficulty with his daughters "North Americanization." They argue frequently, and now they have been withdrawing into silence. The school social worker must be aware of the cultural influences of this family as it relates to attitudes concerning dating and parental compliance. The problem here goes beyond Lourdes's schoolwork. She finds herself in a bicultural conflict: As are many teens in the United States, she is absorbed in dating and boyfriends, while her father believes that young girls should be protected from such contact. In other words, she has acculturated to U.S. culture and her father still refers to his Peruvian culture. Their gap is not only generational, but also cultural. The social worker must be keenly aware of these issues and careful to not alienate either person.

Culture is not the only variable that social workers must take into account. They must also understand the life circumstances of their clients, which may or may not be associated with culture. The social worker must consider these effects when working with clients. For example, there is a high rate of mental disorders among Southeast Asian refugees in the United States. Their conditions have been linked to traumatic life events, such as war, rather than cultural issues per se (Leung & Beohnlein, 1996).

In some cultures, the idea of going to a professional for support or problem solving has negative connotations. Other cultures have a difficult time relating feelings or seeing the purpose of relating feelings. The issue of trust also becomes a principal concern, especially among some ethnic groups who do not have the experience or reference point of going to a helping professional. For example, in the African American culture a common belief holds that counseling or therapy is for "crazy people," and that using mental health services is a sign of weakness of faith. Some may view using the mental health system as giving into the system that has undermined the African American culture (Hines & Boyd-Franklin, 1996). Developing a trusting relationship with a client holding this perspective requires patience on the part of the social worker, and a willingness to step into his or her world. This will require an openness to experiencing and learning about other cultures; the ability to recognize strengths within African American culture; an awareness of the institutional barriers that have historically disenfranchised African Americans; and, knowledge of the verbal and nonverbal messages within African American culture. Box 5.2 presents a variety of intercultural social work experiences.

Box 5.2

Scenario 1. A social worker working with a Vietnamese family from a rural area. The family is concerned about the confidential issues involving their mentally ill adolescent son. The social worker spends a significant time assuring them that confidentiality is an ethic that she will strongly safeguard. Through her training, she is also aware that many Vietnamese will tend to rely on her as a sort of teacher; when appropriate, she will serve this function (Leung & Boehnlein, 1996).

Scenario 2. A social worker in his first job after college works in a rural area where residents are of predominantly Scandinavian descent. Initially, he finds clients to be emotionally closed during counseling sessions. As he gains experience on the job, he realizes that his clients place a high value on the norm of emotional self-control; in response, he develops interviewing strategies that take the norm into account.

Scenario 3. A social worker who does not understand the powerful influence of norms may do severe damage. For instance, telling an Iranian teenager to be more assertive with her father may worsen the relationship, which is based on traditional mores.

Scenario 4. A first-generation Irish family is receptive to taking their problematic child to a family counselor but becomes quite defensive when the social worker confronts them about the dynamics of their marriage. The culturally sensitive social worker will factor this understanding into his or her assessment of the problem and intervention strategies. (McGoldrick, 1996).

When the client's ethnicity is different from the social worker's it is very important that the social worker establish her or his credibility. This requires patience on the part of both client and social worker to work toward an understanding and respect for each other. The social worker, then, must be open to being a student of the client in learning about cultural diversity. At the same time, the social worker must also be careful not to romanticize an ethnic group to the point of failing to recognize pathological perceptions and behaviors. The social worker walks a delicate tightrope in understanding the differences among ethnic groups and also being an effective change agent in empowering clients from diverse cultures.

FOR FURTHER READING

Atkinson, D., & Hackett, G. (1998). *Counseling diverse populations*, 2nd ed. New York: McGraw-Hill.

Atkinson, D., Morton, G., & Sue, D. (1998). *Counseling American minorities*, 5th ed. New York: McGraw-Hill.

Lecca, P., Quervalu, I., Nunes, J. & Gonzales, H. (1998). *Cultural competency in health, social, & human services*. New York: Garland.

WORKBOOK

1. REFLECTION OF FEELING

After reading each item,

a) List four appropriate feeling words; and
b) List your reflection of feeling response, using a different feeling word than one of the four listed below.

Example:

"My Dad and I always fight. He doesn't care about my feelings. He just keeps on accusing me falsely. No matter what I do, he refuses to listen. I just can't win."

a) Feeling words:

i.   **frustrated**
ii.   **hurt**
iii.   **angry**
iv.   **confused**

b) Your feeling response:

You sound very hurt by your Dad. You want things to be better between the two of you.

1. 80-year-old Japanese-American male, talking to the nursing home caseworker.

"This nursing home is not working out. My family is too far away, and I don't know anyone here. I just suffer here alone. The folks here are nice; they are just not family. My daughter and son were planning to come visit me last month, but something came up. I hope that they get here soon—who knows how long I'll last? I wish I knew how to reach my relatives in Japan."

a)   Feeling words:

i.
ii.
iii.
iv.

b)   Your feeling response:

2.   17-year-old female, talking to the school social worker.

"I really want to make the volleyball team. All my friends are varsity players. My grades are too low, even though I've tried really hard to bring them up. The coach wants me to talk to you. He thinks I'm not working hard enough. My parents have put a lot of pressure on me too. I feel really bad about myself. I can't seem to do anything right."

a)   Feeling words:

i.
ii.
iii.
iv.

b)   Your feeling response:

3.   12-year-old male, talking to a hotline worker.

"My Mom and Dad always fight. Sometimes they scream so loud that they wake me up at night. I wish they'd stop it. I lie awake waiting for them to stop. They just keep on and on and on. May be if they didn't live together they'd stop fighting. Is there any hope things will get better?"

a)   Feeling words:

i.
ii.
iii.
iv.

b)   Your feeling response:

4. 23-year-old male, talking to his academic advisor.

"It's not enough that I went to college. I doubt I'll get a job when I graduate. Who would want to hire a person with cerebral palsy! People are uncomfortable around someone like me, stuck in a wheelchair. They don't understand that I'm a very capable worker."

a)   Feeling words:

i.
ii.
iii.
iv.

b)   Your feeling response:

5. A 40-year-old male, talking to a grief counselor.

"My youngest brother was killed in a plane crash. [said in a very angry tone of voice] He was the greatest guy in the world. Where was God? How could God let this happen? My faith had been truly shaken. It's just not fair. I've gone to church to pray, but it doesn't help. Nothing does."

a)   Feeling words:

i.
ii.
iii.
iv.

b)   Your feeling response:

6. A 44-year-old lesbian female, talking to a Child Protective Services caseworker.

    "You are absolutely wrong about me. I don't want to talk to you any more about this. You social workers are all the same. I can't believe you. You must have made a lot of enemies in this business. I would appreciate you leaving me alone. I can manage just fine. I always have, and I always will. Now, if you'd excuse me…"

a)   Feeling words:

i.
ii.
iii.
iv.

b)   Your feeling response:

7. A 68-year-old Dominican male, talking to the senior citizen case manager.

    "Things really are great. My kids are coming here from the Dominican Republic for the holidays, and this new relationship I'm in has my head spinning. I'm so happy and so thankful things have worked out. Five months ago I was considering killing myself. Today I feel great. You have no idea how helpful talking to you has been. Thank you."

a)   Feeling words:

i.
ii.
iii.
iv.

b)   Your feeling response:

8. A 50-year-old female, talking to a domestic violence shelter worker.

"I'm relieved to be out of that violent situation. I was scared for so many years. I hardly know how to act now. I still find myself looking over my shoulder, just waiting for him to find me. But mostly I'm thankful to still be alive."

a)   Feeling words:

i.
ii.
iii.
iv.

b)   Your feeling response:

9. A 24-year-old Mexican-American female, talking to a sexual assault counselor about a sexual assault that occurred eight years ago.

"I was raped when I was in high school. I knew the guy, but we weren't friends. He pretended as if he liked me. I have never told any one because I always felt like somehow I had encouraged him. It wasn't until recently that I've even started to think about what happened. I felt guilty then, but I blocked it out. Now I'm so angry. I feel so violated. It's very difficult to discuss this with my family."

a)   Feeling words:

i.
ii.
iii.
iv.

b)   Your feeling response:

10.   A 25-year-old female, talking to an intake worker at an alcohol treatment center.

"I want to get married to Tom. My parents hate him—because he drinks. I know that he drinks; he's never denied it. So what if he gets out of control occasionally? I grew up in an alcoholic family. It is second nature to me. I know how to handle him. I know how to handle me"

a)   Feeling words:

i.
ii.
iii.
iv.

b)   Your feeling response:

2. PARAPHRASING

Read the following items and identify

a)   The key points in the client's messages (at least 2); and

b)   In your own words, restate what the client has said.

Example:

"I love to play hockey. I love coaching. My kids don't play anymore, but the other kids need me. My wife thinks I should spend more time at home. I don't agree with her. I'm home plenty."

a) Key points in the client's message:

i.   **hockey comes first**

ii.   **disrupting marriage**

iii.   **husband and wife have different expectations**

b) Paraphrasing response:

You enjoy hockey and, it's an important part of your life. You and your wife see this issue differently, which is causing trouble at home.

1. A 40-year-old African-American male, talking to the community mental health clinic caseworker.

    "I really need to talk to my doctor. It's been two weeks since I had my medication. I have to have it now. You don't understand. Without the doctor's okay, I can't get my medicine. The pharmacy closes at five o'clock tonight. It's the only one in town that accepts my medical card. If I don't get my medicine soon, who knows what will happen to me—I need it for my nerves."

a)   Key points in the client's message:

i.   *off his medication*

ii. *in a panic — scared*

iii.

b)   Your paraphrasing response:

2. A Latina mother talking to the school social worker about her 8-year-old son.

"My son, Juanito, was recently diagnosed as having a learning disability. He has a difficult time in school. I know his teachers are frustrated with him, but frankly, I don't think they are doing enough to help him. We've only been in this country for three years; there have been a lot of changes in his life. It's hard for me too, but I try not to dwell on that too much."

a)   Key points in the client's message:

i.

ii.

iii.

b)   Your paraphrasing response:

3. A father talking to the home interventionist about his children.

"I want to get my life back in order. I know I messed up in the past, but I want my kids back. They have been away from me for too long—it's been almost a year. Imagine, strangers raising my kids. I know the foster care system is supposed to help us. Frankly, I think things are much worse since that social worker got involved."

a)   Key points in the client's message:

i.

ii.

iii.

b)   Your paraphrasing response:

4. A 22-year-old female talking to the intake worker at an outpatient treatment program.

"No, I'm not an alcoholic. Sure I drink, everyone I know drinks. It's part of being a college student. The DWI I got last month was no big deal, it was just a stupid mistake. I won't drive after drinking again, that's for sure. Everyone makes my drinking into a major catastrophe. I wish people would back off."

a)   Key points in the client's message:

i.   *feels judged*
ii. *not an alcoholic*
iii. *makes stupid mistakes*

b)   Your paraphrasing response:

5. An 18-year-old male, talking with an adoption specialist about his desire to locate his birth mother.

   "My adoptive parents are great. I know that they love me a lot, and I love them too. But there is this feeling deep inside of me. I want to know who gave birth to me. I want her to tell me why she gave me up. Five years ago, the other social worker told me that I could look for my mom when I was older. Now I'm ready."

a)   Key points in the client's message:

i.
ii.
iii.

b)   Your paraphrasing response:

6. A 35-year-old male, talking about his relationships with friends.

"My friends seem to get bored and tired of me. They go out a lot without me. I find out later, like maybe they've gone to a movie. I call them. I hardly ever get calls back. It's weird. I always end up chasing people down."

a)   Key points in the client's message:

i.   *feels left out*
ii.   *feel you are boring*
iii.

b)   Your paraphrasing response:

7. An 18-year-old college freshman talking to his academic counselor.

"Calculus is really hard for me, but I want to be an engineer. My dad and grandfather are both engineers. They love their work. I've always dreamed of being part of their firm. Now, I'm flunking my major classes and will probably end up on academic probation. My instructor thinks that I may have a learning disability. I don't know…I hate to think I have a problem with my brain."

a)   Key points in the client's message:

i.
ii.
iii.

b)   Your paraphrasing response:

8. A 30-year-old male, talking about the impact of prejudice on his life.

"I was born in Mexico and came to the United States when I was three. People sometimes look at me as if I have no right to be here. I'm an American citizen. I work hard to take care of my family. I'm a part of the community. I just don't understand why people question my place!"

a)   Key points in the client's message:

i.
ii.
iii.

b)   Your paraphrasing response:

9. A 15-year-old female, talking with the school social worker.

"My relationship with my step-dad has always been awkward. I have never felt comfortable around him. He definitely treats his own kids better than he treats me. I'm not saying I'm jealous or anything. In some ways it's easier when he treats me like an acquaintance. Just saying hello and goodbye, and then going our separate ways. But sometimes I wish he'd be proud of me too."

a)   Key points in the client's message:

i.
ii.
iii.

b)   Your paraphrasing response:

10. A 40-year-old female, talking to the intake worker at an eating disorder clinic.

"I've gained 25 pounds in the last 16 months. I try to control my eating habits, but it's hard. I always end up stuffing myself when I feel stressed and overwhelmed. I've tried all the weight loss programs, nothing seems to help. I just keep getting bigger and bigger."

a)   Key points in the client's message:

i.

ii.

iii.

b)   **Your paraphrasing response:**

3. OPEN-ENDED QUESTIONS

After reading each item, identify

a) At least two specific pieces of information that would further your understanding of the problem; and

b) An open-ended question that would prompt the client to provide additional information.

In completing Part b, start by either reflecting the client's feelings or by paraphrasing the content of the client's message, and then ask the open-ended question.

Example:

Client: "I took my medication last night. I didn't want to, but I did. Now I am thinking about whether this is a good idea. I know I am depressed, but I should be able to get through this without drugs."

a) Additional information needed:

i.   **How is the client managing on the medication**
ii.   **Type of medication**
iii.   **Reservations about medication**

b) Your open-ended question:

**You are unsure about whether you want to continue taking the medication. (paraphrase)
What concerns do you have about taking the medication? (open-ended question)**

1. A 50-year-old fundamentalist Christian female, talking with the social worker about her relationship with her daughter.

   "My daughter is living with her boyfriend. We have talked about it a lot. She knows how I feel about her living situation. My religion means everything to me and she knows that too. She is throwing all of her sins in my face. We've never been close, but this felt like the last straw. She is hurting me and hurting God."

a)   Additional information needed:

i.   How long have they been together?
ii.   What is it about the situation you don't like?
iii.

b)   Your open-ended question:

What are some things you've discussed?

Why do you think you aren't close?

How does your daughter feel about your reaction?

2. A 30-year-old male, talking to the social worker about his reactions to a car accident 6 months ago.

"Since my car accident, I'm really afraid to drive again. I get into the car and I feel my heart start to pound and my hands get really sweaty. I don't want to end up behind the wheel and start to panic, but that is what is happening right now. I panic. I've tried to make myself do it, but…I can't. I have flashbacks from the accident; the car turned upside down and I'm trapped inside"

a)   Additional information needed:

i.
ii.
iii.

b)   Your open-ended question:

3. An 80-year-old female, talking to the home interventionist.

"Like I told the other social worker, my children mean the world to me. I'd do anything for them. But I have to draw the line. I can't lend them the money, it would leave me with nothing if I did. I thought once they were adults I wouldn't have to take care of them. Don't they understand that? I'm broke. I can barely make ends meet. This is too much."

a)   Additional information needed:

i.
ii.
iii.

b)   Your open-ended question:

4. A 30-year-old Indian male discussing his relationship with his parents.

"I told my parents that I am gay. They are very traditional, and it's hard talking to them about this. I knew it would freak them out, but I wanted them to meet Michael. We've been together for two years. He's a great person, and I'm finally happy. I just wish they could be happy for me."

a)   Additional information needed:

i.   *What was the conversation like?*

ii. *What their beliefs are?*

iii. *How did they react when they met him?*

b)   Your open-ended question:

What would make your parents happy?

5. A 35-year-old female, talking to the respite care worker about her 5-month-old daughter.

"I have always seen myself as a parent. But how can I be a mom to a child who is mentally retarded? The doctors are of no help to me. This is not the way it's supposed to be. I just feel like I'll never be able to love her the way that I should. Last week, another social worker from the Children's Home came to interview me. She suggested that I meet with you. I know I need the extra help--can't do this alone."

a)   Additional information needed:

i.

ii.

iii.

b)   Your open-ended question:

6. A 17-year-old female, talking to the case manager at the Public Assistance office.

"I'm really excited about having this baby. My boyfriend Dion is giving me a hard time though. He doesn't want the baby. Well…too bad, because I want this baby. I don't need him. We'll be just fine. I've got $400 saved up and a car to get us around. Plus I'm sure that you can help me too."

a)   Additional information needed:

i.
ii.
iii.

b)   Your open-ended question:

7. An 18-year-old female, talking to the school social worker.

"I am the youngest of seven children. Sometimes I feel invisible. Sometimes I feel smothered. My oldest sister has always acted like she's my mom. I guess that makes me really mad. Plus, mom shows up when she feels like it, and that makes me angry too. I want to have a normal family when I get married."

a)   Additional information needed:

i.
ii.
iii.

b)   Your open-ended question:

8. A 50-year-old male, discussing his home situation with the Employee Assistance Program social worker.

"I love watching movies. It's the best way for me to relax. I can get away from the craziness of my day. My wife gets mad, though. She expects me to be more involved with the kids. I can't be with them when I feel so torn up inside. There's so much pressure. I'm supporting the family, helping out with my parents, and trying to keep my job."

a)   Additional information needed:

i.
ii.
iii.

b)   Your open-ended question:

9. A 30-year-old female, discussing her reactions to the sexual assault survivors group.

"This support group is not working for me. People in the group just come here to complain about their terrible lives. I want to move on with my life and not stay stuck in my misery. I feel like if I continue to come here, it will wear me down completely."

a)   Additional information needed:

i.
ii.
iii.

b)   Your open-ended question:

10. A 15-year-old Native American female, talking to an outreach worker.

"I've never had much to do with my Mom, and now my Grandmother is very sick. She is the most important person in my life. I couldn't bear it if something happened to her. I know I'm only 15, but I'd rather be on my own than have to stay with my Mom. I doubt she'd want me to live with her anyway."

a)   Additional information needed:

i.
ii.
iii.

b)   Your open-ended question:

4. CLOSED-ENDED QUESTIONS

Read the items listed below and identify

a) At least two specific pieces of information that would further your understanding of the problem; and
b) A closed-ended question that would prompt the client to provide additional information.

Example:

A 29-year-old male, talking to the outreach caseworker.

"I moved to this country from Argentina. I like it here, but I miss my family."

a) Specific information needed:

i.   **How long has the client lived here?**
ii.   **Who is still in Argentina?**
iii.   **Who is here with the client?**

b) Closed-ended question:

   How long have you been in the United States?

1. A 14-year-old Japanese American male, talking to the school social worker about his difficulties at school.

   "I've never gotten into trouble at school. I wish the teachers would all drop dead. This one time I messed up and now I'm busted. Here I am talking to you. My parents are going to freak. They are not going to understand. Is this a drag or what?"

a)   Specific information needed:

i.
ii.
iii.

b)   Your closed-ended question:

2. A 10-year-old White female, talking to her outreach worker.

"My mom yells at me a lot. Sometimes she's nice, sometimes she's mean. I never know which way she's going to be. I try to do things right, so she doesn't get mad at me. I hope she'll be nice to me after my meeting with you is over. She didn't like it when that social worker from Child Welfare came to our house."

a)   Specific information needed:

i.
ii.
iii.

b)   Your closed-ended question:

3. A 16-year-old African American female, talking to the group home social worker.

"Everyone gets to go to the concert but me. The staffers here at the group home are so strict. They never let me go out with my friends. They practically keep me locked up in my room. I hate being here, jail would be better."

a)   Specific information needed:

i.
ii.
iii.

b)   Your closed-ended question:

4. A 65-year-old female, talking to the caseworker at the senior citizens center.

    "We've been together for a long time. You would think by now my children would accept our marriage. They pretend like my husband doesn't exist. I want them to get along. Is that too much to ask? Sometimes I feel like they treat me as a child."

a)   Specific information needed:

i.
ii.
iii.

b)   Your closed-ended question:

5. A 35-year-old Hispanic female, talking to the community organization representative about her living situation.

    "My landlord has great plans for this building. Those plans include kicking us out so he can renovate the place and charge a higher rent. We would never be able to afford it. I don't have an extra dime at the end of the month. I've always kept the place nice and paid my rent on time. I have no where else to go. It is so unfair. I hope that you will be able to help me."

a) Specific information needed:

i.
ii.
iii.

b)   Your closed-ended question:

6. A 17-year-old female, talking to the case manager about her pregnancy.

"I'm three months pregnant and I don't know what to do. I'm not sure who the father is. I need help, I can't believe I got myself into this mess."

a)   Specific information needed:

i.
ii.
iii.

b)   Your closed-ended question:

7. A 20-year-old African American male, talking to his college counselor.

"I got a full scholarship for the next year. I worked so hard. I gave up everything in my life, my friends, my job, to win it. Now I feel let down—it's like nothing will ever satisfy me. I go for the top achievement, but once I get there it's never enough for me to be happy. I want to feel a sense of accomplishment. All I feel right now is a giant hole. Sometimes I feel selfish because my parents never had the opportunity to go to college."

a)   Specific information needed:

i.
ii.
iii.

b)   Your closed-ended question:

8. A 25-year-old White female, talking to the social worker in the eating disorder clinic.

    "Of course I eat properly. My parents and boyfriend are the ones who have a problem with my weight. They are completely obsessed with how I look and what I eat. It's really none of their business. I feel fine, I don't see any reason to talk about this with you or them."

a)   Specific information needed:

i.
ii.
iii.

b)   Your closed-ended question:

9. A 55-year-old HIV-positive male, talking to a home interventionist social worker about his medical problems.

    "I take anti-viral medication on a regular basis. When my T-cell count is stable, I feel much better. I just wish I didn't have HIV. It's awful."

a)   Specific information needed:

i.
ii.
iii.

b)   Your closed-ended question:

10. A 75-year-old Hispanic male, talking about faith with the hospice social worker.

"My religion has always been a source of comfort to me. No matter what the problem, I've always turned to prayer during the rough times. People think I'm crazy, but I'm leaving my fate up to God. No more medicine, no more doctors."

a)   Specific information needed:

i.
ii.
iii.

b)   Your closed-ended question:

5. CLARIFICATION

Read the following items and identify

a) Information that needs to be made clearer (at least two); and
b) A clarifying response.

Example:

"No matter how hard I try, they always yell at me."

a) What needs to be clearer:

i.   **Who are they?**
ii.   **How often is always?**

b) Clarifying response:

When you say "they," whom do you mean?

1. A 40-year-old Puerto-Rican female, talking to an outreach caseworker.

"We're going to be evicted, I just know it. We have no money and I don't know what to do next. My parents said we couldn't live with them. I've got my kids to worry about too. I came here from Puerto Rico for a better life, but I'm still in the same situation."

a) What information needs to be clearer?

i.
ii.

b) Your clarifying response:

2. A 34-year-oldWhite female, talking to the home interventionist caseworker.

"I admit that the kids are fighting all the time. My husband wants me to settle it, but I don't see that as my job. I end up sticking up for them, which really makes him mad. I can't seem to win. I hate that I can't handle this on my own, that I have to meet with you. Here I am in the middle again."

    a) What information needs to be clearer?

    i.
    ii.

    b) Your clarifying response:

3. A 16-year-old White male, talking to the caseworker from the Child Protection Agency.

"So what if it's illegal! We got really high last night. It was a great time. I love being high. I can forget all my worries. You social workers are all alike, trying to tell me what to do."

    a) What information needs to be clearer?

    i. *What's illegal?*
    ii. *Who's we?*

    b) Your clarifying response:

4. A 25-year-old White female, talking to the Employee Assistance Program social worker about frustrations related to her job.

    "I've been working at this job for five years and the crap I have to put up with! My boss always singles me out and criticizes me in front of my coworkers. Can you believe that? Five years! Five long years!"

    a) What information needs to be clearer?

      i. *How does he single you out?*
      ii. *How does he criticize?*

    b) Your clarifying response:

5. A 35-year-old White male, talking to his academic advisor.

    "I'm trying hard to understand these chemistry problems. I was never a very good student, especially in science. Now here I am, 35 years old and back in college. I'll never get through this. Some of my family is behind me, and I don't want to let them down."

    a) What information needs to be clearer?

    i.
    ii.

    b) Your clarifying response:

6. A 38-year-old White female, talking to a sexual abuse counselor.

"My grandfather did awful and disgusting things to me when I was young. He made me promise not to tell my parents which I never did. Now I'm a mom myself, and I can't stop thinking about him and what happened."

    a) What information needs to be clearer?

    i.
    ii.

    b) Your clarifying response:

7. A 15-year-old African American male, talking to his foster care caseworker.

"I've never liked living with this foster family. They just seem to "put up" with me. My foster brother, Jimmy, is picking on me all the time, and he makes fun of me, especially at school. Could you please find me a new family? I don't think I can take it any more."

    a) What information needs to be clearer:

    i.   *How does he pick on you?*
    ii. *What does "put up" with mean?*

    b) Your clarifying response:

8. A 25-year-old White male, talking to a caseworker about his social relationships.

"I have a lot of trouble saying no. People always ask me to do them favors I don't want to do, but I wind up doing them anyway. I've always been this way. I always end up with a sick feeling in my stomach."

    a) What information needs to be clearer:

    i.
    ii.

    b) Your clarifying response:

9. A 40-year-old White male talking to a community-based social worker about his father.

"I grew up in a troubled family. My Dad has been in and out of mental institutions and prisons most of his life. I never really had a chance to get to know him. Now he's being released, and he'll be living in a halfway house. Someone is supposed to meet with me next week to help me figure out what other resources he'll need. I don't know what to do, and I don't know how I feel about all of this coming down on me."

    a) What information needs to be clearer?

    i.
    ii.

    b) Your clarifying response:

10. A 30-year-old female, talking to an intake worker at the local soup kitchen. "We've been living on the streets for a couple of months. My kids and I sleep at the shelter; sometimes we eat there. Summer is almost over, which means that life gets even harder."

a) What information needs to be clearer?

i.
ii.

b) Your clarifying response:

ს. ᲔMMARIZATION

Read the following vignettes and

a) Identify **at least two** key aspects of the client's statement; and
b) Provide a summarization response to the client's entire statement.

Example:

A 40-year-old White male talking with a caseworker at the domestic violence prevention center.

Social worker:	**So, tell me more about your experience in the support group. I know you've been attending the sessions for the past 12 weeks.**
Client:	**Well, it's okay. Most of the guys are a lot like me. We want our wives to stay home with the kids. Things would be better if my wife listened to me and stopped riding me so much.**
Social worker:	**You want Leslie to back off and give you some breathing room.**
Client:	**Definitely. She does things that aggravate me. Sometimes it feels as if she purposefully pisses me off. Like she's just waiting to see what I'll do next.**
Social worker:	**What happens at those times?**
Client:	**It depends. Sometimes I yell. Most of the time I leave now. I know that if I stick around, I'm likely to do something that I'll regret, maybe hit her.**

a)   Most important aspects of the client's statement:

  i.   **He attends a batterers support group.**
  ii.   **He feels as if his wife is purposefully testing him.**
  iii.   **He has seen some change in his behavior since attending the group.**

b)   Your summarization response based on the entire dialogue:

  Now-you are able to identify certain situations that could lead to hurting Leslie. Through the help of the support group, you're learning other ways of dealing with your wife.

Case #1:

A 40-year-old overweight female talks with an intake social worker about her failures and loneliness.

SW	Jeanne, let's talk for a minute about some of the things that are bothering you.
CL:	My weight. I guess it's all cyclical. I mean being overweight, not a lot of people want to be your friend. I feel lonely. I've always felt rejected since I was little.
SW:	It's hard for you to remember a time when you felt as though you belonged?
CL:	Yeah. I feel crappy about myself. Lonely. I don't make any friends. I hurt the people who actually do love me. I let down my family all the time.
SW:	Tell me about that. How do you let your family down?
CL:	Well, they always try to build me up. They support me. When I quit school, I knew it hurt them. I work at a Laundromat, I'm sure they want more for me than that. I guess I was never motivated enough to learn another trade. So I work in a Laundromat, and I guess I do okay there. I don't know.

a)   Most important aspects of the client's statement:

   i.
   ii.
   iii.

b)   Your summarization response, based on the entire dialogue:

Case #2:

A 60-year-old female talking with the hospital social worker. She is considering suicide after recently learning that she has terminal cancer.

CL: The news is terminal cancer, so I am not going to live like this! I don't want to feel myself dying every day. I think I'm just going to take care of it on my own.

SW: What do you mean, "take care of it"?

CL: I think I'm just going to go off on my own, and whatever happens, happens. I don't want to live. I don't want to end up incapable of taking care of myself. I'm going to die anyway. I'll say my good-byes while I'm okay.

SW: You feel hopeless about what the future holds.

CL: Yeah, I do. I've always had a full life. Lots of friends. My family is the best. How can I put them through my slow and painful death? I don't want to burden anyone with caring for me. It would be so unfair.

a)   Most important aspects of the client's statement:

       i.
       ii.
       iii.

b)   Your summarization response, based on the entire dialogue:

<u>Case #3</u>:

A 75-year-old African-American female who is living in a nursing home. She wants to go back home, but her children feel strongly that this is her only option.

SW: Eleanor, you've been at the nursing home for the past six months. I know that at times you've been very unhappy here. How have you been doing recently?

CL: Well, I just hate it here. I absolutely hate it here. My roommate, Emma, cries all the time. There's not a moment's peace. I get hungry, and I can't eat. I can't eat until they come get us for breakfast, lunch and supper. My kids haven't been here to see me in three months. I'm really lonely. I just hate it here.

SW: As time wears on, it's even harder for you to make peace with being here?

CL: Yes, it is just getting worse. I don't see it ever getting better. I hate being here. It's really depressing and I was happier before I came. I had the fall and broke my hip and, next thing you know, here I am. I have my wits about me. I know who I am and I feel like I can take care of myself. I just don't feel like I belong here.

SW: I know it's been very hard for you, but from talking with your son and daughter, they feel it's not possible for you to go home. There's just no help available.

CL: Well, I just don't think they give me enough credit. I think that I could take care of myself and that I would not need somebody with me 24 **hours** a day. I don't know why they think that. I just feel like they're throwing me away.

SW: They don't see your strength? That you are capable of managing with some assistance?

CL: I realize that when I first broke my hip, I was incapacitated and was not able to do for myself. But I'm better, and I'm getting around with my walker. And there are many things I can do by myself now.

a)   Most important aspects of the client's statement:

      i.

      ii.

      iii.

b)   Your summarization response, based on the entire dialogue:

Case #4:

A 17-year-old White male, talking to the school social worker. He is considering dropping out of school.

SW: I know this is a really big decision for you, whether or not to stay in school.

CL: It's just those teachers, the homework, and the tests. It's just everything. I've pretty much come to a conclusion that school's got nothing to do with the real world. I'm sitting here learning about geography, snow glaciers, and what does this have to do with life, with the outside world? I think I've had enough. It's the conformity, and the structure, and all the rules. I'm thinking about quitting. A friend of mine quit. He's not employed right now; but he's doing okay. Not that I want to be a brain surgeon or anything. I just want to get a good job, and pay my bills, and to live on my own.

SW: What would you do if you quit school?

CL: I'd get a job. I don't know. Maybe just hang out for awhile. I could use the break.

a)   Most important aspects of the client's statement:

      i.

      ii.

      iii.

b)   Your summarization response, based on the entire dialogue:

Case #5:

A 40-year-old male, talking to a hotline worker. He is a single parent with two teenage daughters, and is feeling overwhelmed.

CL: Being a single parent and having two teenage daughters isn't the easiest thing in the world, I tell you. They are rebellious. They use the phone a lot. They're coming home later and later. I want to give them their space, they're individuals. But I'm worried about them too.

SW: You sound like you're concerned about your girls and also realistic, knowing that part of being a teenager is having some freedom.

CL: Recently, I gave them a curfew and they are furious with me. They say, "Dad, you're not being fair. You're being too strict with us." Well, I don't want them out at all hours of the night. I want them to respect the rules of the house. They respect me, and I respect them.

SW: That's very reasonable. You are the parent.

CL: It's not reasonable in their eyes, and we have been getting into fights. And it's just chaos. And I really wish my wife was still alive, because it's a lot for one parent. I guess dads and daughters are a struggle. It's a struggle.

a)   Most important aspects of the client's statement:

      i.
      ii.
      iii.

b)   Your summarization response, based on the entire dialogue:

Case #6:

A 22-year-old African American female who won't be graduating with her class. Her mother is supporting her financially. She is talking to her college counselor.

SW: Kamaria, the last time we met, we spent time talking about your
                 frustration at not graduating on time. We agreed that we would talk more
                 about that today. Where do you want to start?

CL: Well, I'm still feeling like I'm letting my Mom down and that I should be
                 graduating this May. And that upsets me, and it makes me feel like I'm not
                 doing what I should. My Mom tells me, "Don't worry about it, everybody
                 does things in their own time." I know that when she was in school, she
                 finished...she went to a two-year college, and then came here. Plus, she
                 had me. She graduated from here and she finished on time. I don't have
                 any children, I don't have anything to set me back. It's just me. And it's
                 gonna take me longer than it took her. I don't have those obstacles
                 standing in my way and I'm still not where I think I'm supposed to be. I
                 feel bad about that.

SW: Sounds like you feel guilty.

CL: I do. I don't have any of the complications that she did. The only
                 responsibilities I have are credit card bills. So I work part time. I should be
                 graduating in May. She says I haven't let her down, but I still feel like I
                 have. She tells me that I don't have to live up to anybody's standards, but I
                 feel like I'm letting myself down too.

a)   Most important aspects of the client's statement:

       i.
       ii.
       iii.

b)   Your summarization response, based on the entire dialogue:

Case #7:

A 23-year-old White male who recently ended a relationship with his girlfriend. She has
attempted suicide and he feels responsible.

CL: I thought things were over. Then she called me again on Monday.

SW: Just two days ago?

CL: Right. Well, yeah. It's been OVER for me. I thought it was over for her too.

W: These last three months have been up and down, things change from minute to minute.

CL: Yeah.

SW: David, what's your take on her suicide attempt?

CL: Well, a couple days before the suicide attempt, we had a party at my house. I was running around trying to keep the house organized. And she kept yelling at me, "David, why don't you hang out with me?" Well, she got really upset with me, and trashed my room. We got into an argument out in the parking lot. She grabbed me tightly. I still have some marks on my arms from a fight two months ago. I said, "Stop, you're getting violent." She said, "I'll show you what violent is." I walked away, and she got down on her knees and banged her head on the concrete.

SW: That must have been very frightening for you.

CL: It was. I don't know what my take is on this. I think she needs help, but I can't help her. I have too much going on in my life. I care for her, but I've done my part. I called the Crisis Hotline and her parents.

a)   Most important aspects of the client's statement:

       i.
       ii.
       iii.

b)   Your summarization response, based on the entire dialogue:

#8: Continued with David- Session #2

SW: David, we spent our last session talking about Lisa, your ex-girlfriend who was very abusive to you. When we ended, we talked about exploring other relationships that you've been in and how you tend to get into relationships with females that are not necessarily good for you.

CL: Well, I think it started with my first girlfriend, my freshman year in high school. I was nice to her. When I broke up with her, she tried to kill herself. I felt like it was my fault. Then, I dated a couple of people off and on. I had a really great relationship my senior year in high school. It lasted for a year or so. It was really good until we went away to college. And after that, I really haven't met any girls who have been very stable.

SW: It seems as if you are questioning for yourself...What is it that attracts these women to me or me to them? How can I make better choices in a relationship?

CL: Yeah! The thing I keep finding out about myself is that I'm too nice. I don't want people to be mad at me. I'll do anything for anyone.

SW: What do you mean when you say "I'm too nice"?

CL: Just that I'll do whatever anybody wants me to. I want people, especially girls, to like me. Even if it means I get hurt. I know it sounds crazy.

a)   Most important aspects of the client's statement:

    i.
    ii.
    iii.

b)   Your summarization response, based on the entire dialogue:

CASE #9:

A 33-year-old White male, talking to his caseworker at the day treatment program. He is chronically depressed and is not taking his medication.

SW: You know, Tony, we've been talking a lot about your medication, and you said that you would make a commitment to take your medication every day.

CL: Right. I know if I don't take my medication, I get very depressed. And I've been depressed all week. I've been slipping, taking my medication. So I think that I need to be on a very strict regimen.

SW: When do you take your medication?

CL: Well, I'm supposed to take it three times a day: in the morning; at noon, and right after dinner. You know, if I'm out with my friends, it's a struggle for me to take it. I get lazy. I understand the importance. I just need, I guess, to be more structured. I know that when I come in here, I always promise you that I am going to do everything on the treatment plan, and I screw up. I don't want to do that anymore. I didn't like myself this week. I scared myself. I was really, really depressed.

a)   Most important aspects of the client's statement:

   i.
   ii.
   iii.

b)   Your summarization response, based on the entire dialogue:

CASE #10:

An 18-year-old White female, talking to a probation officer. She was recently arrested on drug charges. She denies that she's addicted to drugs, but acknowledges that she's afraid of the legal consequences.

SW: What happened after you were arrested for possession of illegal drugs?

CL: Well, my Mom and Stepdad came and bailed me out of jail. I've got a public defender and I go to court in a couple of months. I got caught with cocaine. It wasn't very much; it was less than a gram. But it seems that cocaine, any possession of any of it, is a felony offense. So I'm concerned about that. And my parents are really pissed off. They didn't really know that I was involved in drugs. They're real freaked out and they want me to go into treatment. I don't think that's necessary because I don't have a drug problem.

SW: As you see it, you're not concerned about your drug usage, just the possible legal consequences.

CL: I suppose, yeah. I don't want to end up spending time in prison. I couldn't hack that. Plus my parents are threatening me, too. It just seems like they're always surprised. Each time they find out about something new, something "bad," they're shocked.

a)   Most important aspects of the client's statement:

      i.
      ii.
      iii.

b)   Your summarization response, based on the entire dialogue:

7. INFORMATION GIVING

After reading each item, complete the following:

a) Generalize the problem (in universal or global terms);
b) Identify the most important pieces of information in the client's statement (at least two); and
c) Provide an information-giving response.

Example:

A 41-year-old female, talking to a hospital social worker about her inability to get pregnant.

Client: "I'm devastated. I want to have a family. My husband and I tried every medical procedure possible. We've spent all our savings; plus, it seems like we've talked to every specialist in the state. We have reached the end. We agreed if I wasn't pregnant by the time I turned 40, we would give up."

a)   Generalize the problem:

There are significant constraints related to getting pregnant at age 40. Anger and disappointment are normal feelings.

b)   Most important pieces of information:

i.   **They have spent all their savings in an effort to have a baby**
ii.   **Time is also running out**
iii.   **Feelings (disappointed, frustrated, anxious)**

c)   Your information-giving response:

It's understandable that you feel angry and disappointed, after so many unsuccessful attempts at getting pregnant. Maybe looking into some other options, such as adoption, might be a next step.

1.   A 37-year-old White male, talking to a hotline worker about his marriage.

"I think my wife is having an affair. She hasn't said it in so many words, but I can just tell. She's not home much and when she is, she seems miles away. She is beautiful and any guy would love to have her on his arm. I don't know how to ask her or even if I want to know. We've been married for seven years--some times have been better than others. This is the first time I've felt so scared."

a)   Generalize the problem:

b)   Most important pieces of information:

i.
ii.
iii.

c)   Your information-giving response:

2. A 40-year-old White female, talking about her alcohol usage to an intake caseworker.

"I drink a lot. I don't deny that, but an alcoholic, that's a joke. Alcoholics are bums on the street, drinking a bottle of whisky out of a brown paper bag. My father, now *he* was an alcoholic. He'd leave for days at a time, and he never held down a job. He was a loser who never amounted to anything. I have a good job. I make decent money. There has never been a time that I haven't been able to control my drinking. Do I fit the alcohol profile?"

a)   Generalize the problem:

b)   Most important pieces of information:

i.
ii.
iii.

c)   Your information-giving response:

3. A 12-year-old girl, talking to the community outreach worker about her mother.

"My mother was diagnosed as having schizophrenia when I was two. I don't know what that means, exactly, but she does weird things. She believes that people are following us, and sometimes she hears voices. My Dad doesn't want to talk to me about why my Mom acts so strange. He says I'm too young to understand. Is this schizophrenia thing hereditary? Will I end up like her?"

a)   Generalize the problem:

b)   Most important pieces of information:

i.
ii.
iii.

c)   Your information-giving response:

4. A 22-year-old Italian American female, talking with another social work student about her guilt surrounding a cousin's sexual victimization.

"I knew my cousin was being molested by her father. She kind of hinted about it when we were younger, maybe 10 or so. Now I am in social work classes, and we are learning about sexual abuse. I should have done something then. Now I feel so guilty for doing nothing."

a)   Generalize the problem:

b)   Most important pieces of information:

i.
ii.
iii.

c)   Your information-giving response:

5. A 21-year-old male, talking with a crisis counselor on the hotline.

"I'll never feel okay again. Losing my Dad, having him die so unexpectedly, leaves me with no chance to say goodbye. He wouldn't want me to drop out of school, but I don't have the strength to keep up with my work or the motivation to study. I always counted on him, and now he's gone. I'm at such a loss. How do people get through this?"

a)   Generalize the problem:

b)   Most important pieces of information:

i.
ii.
iii.

c)   Your information-giving response:

6. A 25-year-old female, talking to the domestic violence shelter intake worker.

"Last night, I was beaten up by my boyfriend. This is probably the fourth or fifth time. He treated me nicely when we first met, but now he gets so jealous. He refuses to let me see my friends or Mom, and I'm sure he followed me home from work last night. He's starting to really scare me. That's why I came to the shelter."

a)   Generalize the problem:

b)   Most important pieces of information:

i.
ii.
iii.

c)   Your information giving response:

7. A 17-year-old female, talking with a Child Protection Service social worker.

"I told that other social worker, the one at school, that I don't use drugs that often and frankly this is my body and my baby. I appreciate your concern, but it's none of your business. I'm 17, and old enough to make my own decisions. It pisses me off that now Child Protection Services is involved. It's my life, my child, my choice."

a)   Generalize the problem:

b)   Most important pieces of information:

i.
ii.
iii.

c)   Your information-giving response:

8. A 70-year-old man, talking to the hospital social worker about his finances and future.

"My wife and I need help. Everyone says, "Go talk to the social worker." We're just about broke, and with my wife here in the hospital, we can't pay for all her medical bills or get help once she gets home. She had a stroke, so she'll need a lot of care, but...I don't want her going into a nursing home, no matter what. She wouldn't want that either."

a)   Generalize the problem:

b)   Most important pieces of information:

i.
ii.
iii.

c)   Your information giving response:

9. A 10-year-old girl, talking with the school social worker.

"Last week my parents told us they're getting a divorce. It's been coming for a long time, but I really want them to stay together. My sister says there is no chance of them staying married, but I don't believe that. Please give me some ideas about how I can prevent this from happening."

a)   Generalize the problem:

b)   Most important pieces of information:

i.

ii.
iii.

c)   Your information-giving response:

10. A mother talking to the school social worker about her 6-year-old daughter.

"My daughter is having such a hard time making friends. She's so demanding and bossy to everyone. She's always been like this, but since her brother was born, it's gotten much worse. At school Susie spends most of her time alone now—the other kids want nothing to do with her. I've tried every thing I can think of, but she's driving me crazy. Her teacher suggested that I talk to you."

a)   Generalize the problem:

b)   Most important pieces of information:

i.
ii.
iii.

c)   Your information-giving response:

8. INTERPRETATION

Read the following items and identify:

a) At least two underlying issues that need to be addressed; and
b) Your interpretive response.

Example:

A 28-year-old woman is currently in a violent relationship. She informs you that she doesn't mind a few punches now and then. "It's better than being alone." She's been in two other relationships, both of which were violent.

a)   What underlying issues should be addressed? (at least two)

i.   **pattern of abuse**
ii.   **self-esteem**
iii.   **fear of being alone**

b)   Interpretative response.

        I get the sense that somehow that you feel you deserve to be abused, that you're not worth being treated with respect.

1   A 45-year-old man who is currently unemployed reports that he is looking for work, but no one is hiring a "middle-aged has-been." He also reports that there have been other times in his life when he has been unemployed for over six months. He was a midlevel manager at a fire company prior to his layoff. He is the sole financial support for his family.

a)   What underlying issues would you address?

i.   *feelings of worthlessness*
ii. *feels old*
iii. *scared*

b)   Your interpretative response.

        I get the feeling you worry about supporting your family & that you won't ever be hired again. You were unemployed before, but you got out of it.

2   A 56-year-old woman is currently the sole caretaker of her elderly parents. Her mother, age 85, is able to manage fairly well. Her father, age 85, has been diagnosed with Alzheimer's

Disease and is no longer able to recognize his family. Your client refuses to place him in a nursing home, stating "He'd never forgive me. Finally, after all these years, I'm able to repay him for all the trouble I caused. I never was the daughter he was proud of. My sister, the perfect one, is now nowhere to be found. I guess she's too busy." [stated softly]

a)   What underlying issues would you address?

i.
ii.
iii.

b)   Your interpretative response.

3   A 14-year-old girl who has always excelled in her academic classes recently has refused to answer questions during class and no longer completes homework assignments. She appears uninterested in any school activities and states "I'm tired of sticking out. I hate people thinking that I'm the school brain."

a)   What underlying issues would you address?

i.
ii.
iii.

b)   Your interpretative response.

4   A 35-year-old woman, who is a single parent, reports that her 8-year-old daughter, Karen, has refused to go to school for the past 4 weeks. Recently the mother has decided "not to force the issue" because it's been nice having her company at home. She's now thinking about home schooling.

a)   What underlying issues would you address?

i.
ii.
iii.

b)   Your interpretative response.

5   A 25-year-old man is considering leaving his job as a social worker and joining the priesthood. He has always felt a "calling" to help others and believes that he can best fulfill that need through his religion. Recently he ended a five-year relationship with his college sweetheart who is "pressuring me into getting married."

a)   What underlying issues would you address?

i.
ii.
iii.

b)   Your interpretative response.

6   A 62-year-old divorced man has made the decision to retire after a successful career as an architect. He reports that he wants to sell his company, but has yet to find the "right buyer." He acknowledges that he has always focused on his career and doesn't have many outside interests or hobbies. His daughter, recently widowed with two children, would like him to move to Chicago and "help her get back on her feet." His relationship with her has been strained since he divorced her mother 15 years ago.

a)   What underlying issues would you address?

i.
ii.
iii.

b)   Your interpretative response.

7 A 30-year-old single woman reports that she loves children, wants to get married, and "have it all." She has been in several relationships during the past 10 years and has turned down two marriage proposals. The product of divorced parents, she feels it is essential to be "absolutely sure." She is waiting until the "perfect person" comes into her life. She also states that her younger brother is gay. She's sure it's because of all the conflicts between her parents while they were growing up that he's now a homosexual.

a)   What underlying issues would you address?

i.
ii.
iii.

b)   Your interpretative response.

8 A 48-year-old man is currently attending an outpatient alcohol and drug treatment program. He reports having trouble staying sober. Recently his wife was promoted and she is now an executive at a major corporation. He is very proud of her accomplishments, but in a passing comment he states "I wish it was me. I've worked hard all my life, but she deserves the glory."

a)   What underlying issues would you address?

i.
ii.
iii.

b)   Your interpretative response.

9 A 30-year-old woman reports that her best friend has no time for her anymore, now that she has a boyfriend. Although she would like to be in a relationship, she doesn't want to get hurt. Her pattern of behaviors includes excessive jealousy; saying one thing yet doing something else; and "testing" the other person. She states that it is hard for her to trust people, especially men. She's afraid they'll leave her too, "just like my Dad did."

a)   What underlying issues would you address?

i.
ii.
iii.

b)   Your interpretative response.

10 A 37-year-old man who was recently diagnosed with cancer. He has started chemotherapy
    and is experiencing debilitating side effects. His physician reports that the prognosis for this
    client is very promising, but he must continue with the treatment. The client is unsure about
    whether he can handle all the struggles associated with his treatment. He states that he never
    imagined being so scared and wonders whether he'll ever feel like himself again. His wife is
    very supportive, but tends not to assert herself in their relationship. He has always been the
    decision-maker.

a)   What underlying issues would you address?

i.
ii.
iii.

b)   Your interpretative response.

9. CONFRONTATION

Read the following items and identify:

a) Issues you would address related to the problem (at least two); and
b) Your confrontational response

Example:

A 26-year-old female has expressed an interest in working on improving her relationships with people in her life. The client has informed the social worker that she can only meet at 1:00 p.m. on Wednesday. For the past two weeks she has come at 1:15 p.m. and today she did not attend at all.

a)   What issues would you address?

i.   **Her lateness**
ii.   **Does she really want to be in counseling?**
iii.   **What seems to be getting in the way of her attending the counseling sessions?**

b)   Confrontational response:

I'm concerned that you have either been late for our sessions or not coming at all. You have asked to meet on Wednesdays and you are not following through. I wonder if you are truly committed to this process.

1. A 38-year-old male is fighting for greater visitation rights with his two children. He has shared with the social worker that he is having a sexual relationship with a coworker. The divorce decree states that he is not to have any overnight guests while the children are with him. He also reports that his ex-wife plans to take him back to court. She wants the judge to order only "supervised visits" until the children are older (they are 6 and 10).

a)   What issues would you address?

i.

ii.

iii.

b)   Your confrontational response:

2. A 17-year-old female who is 4 months pregnant comes to your agency, stating that she wants to keep the baby. She is excited about becoming a parent. During her session, she casually mentions that she is drinking alcohol and smoking marijuana. She reports that she feels good most of the time, but has recently been experiencing low energy and a loss of appetite.

a)   What issues would you address?

i.
ii.
iii.

b)   Your confrontational response:

3. A 14-year-old male was caught breaking and entering into a local business. This is his second offense. He is on probation and there is a good possibility of serving time in a juvenile facility. He appears to be fairly confident that nothing is going to happen.

a)   What issues would you address?

i.
ii.
iii.

b)   Your confrontational response:

4. A 48-year-old male who has experienced multiple sexual relationships. He states that he is careful in selecting partners, and always asks if they have been exposed to AIDS. He uses protection periodically. He enjoys his freedom and sees nothing problematic about his behavior.

a)   What issues would you address?

i.

ii.

iii.

b)   Your confrontational response:

5. A 30-year-old female has been married for five years to a controlling man. She recently lost
    20 pounds because her husband told her she was too fat. Although she wants a child, she
    agreed not to get pregnant because she would no longer be physically attractive to him.

a)   What issues would you address?

i.

ii.

iii.

b)   Your confrontational response:

Is it (the marriage) worth all these sacrifices?

6   A 45-year-old male who is schizophrenic refuses to take his anti-psychotic medication
    because the side effects include headaches and nausea. He states that he has experienced long
    periods of feeling fine and has no need to take the medication. The staff at his current day
    treatment program has informed you that he must continue taking his medication or he will
    be terminated from the program.

a)   What issues would you address?

i.

ii.

iii.

b)   Your confrontational response:

7. A 35-year-old woman admits to physically abusing her children, ages 8 and 12. She reports that she has taken parenting classes and has learned "time-out" procedures. During a family session, you observe the client raising her voice and threatening to hurt her eldest daughter.

a)   What issues would you address?

i.
ii.
iii.

b)   Your confrontational response:

8. An 18-year-old college student, who has a four-year scholarship, is currently failing all of his classes. He reports that his instructors are hard on him and expect too much from freshmen. He did exceptionally well academically in high school and was the star of his football team. Recently he stopped going to all of his classes, stating that "It's a lost cause." He reports that next year he will attend the community college at home and live with his parents. As he continues talking, tears are running down his face.

a)   What issues would you address?

i.
ii.
iii.

b)   Your confrontational response:

9. A 20-year-old female college student admits to having "weird eating habits." She eats one piece of toast for breakfast and a cup of soup for dinner. She is proud of her ability to limit her food intake and has lost 10 pounds in the last two weeks.

a) What issues would you address?

i.
ii.
iii.

b) Your confrontational response:

10. A 13-year-old girl is currently living in a foster home. During a weekend visit with her mother, she ran away. Two days later, she was picked up by the police. She reports that she ran away from home because she didn't want to go back to the foster family. Her plan is to keep running until she can live permanently with her mother.

a) What issues would you address?

i.
ii.
iii.

b) Your confrontational response:

10. PITFALLS

In this section, you are presented with 14 scenarios. All of them have at least two problematic social worker responses. Read each case and complete the following:

a) In your own words, identify the mistakes that are made;
b) Explain why those problematic responses could lead to barriers in furthering the relationship; and
c) Provide a correct social worker response.

In completing these exercises, you may want to refer to this list of pitfalls covered in the CD-ROM:

- advice giving;
- inappropriate use of humor;
- interrupting the client/abrupt transitions;
- judgmental response;
- offering false assurance;
- premature confrontation
- inappropriate self-disclosure by the social worker;
- overwhelming the client with too much information;
- premature problem solving;
- insincerity/lack of genuineness;
- minimizing the problem.

Example:

The client is a 38-year-old female who has just miscarried for the third time.

Client:	**This is awful. Three miscarriages, and my husband and I really want a baby. And I just feel, I don't know, if I'm paying for something that I have done before. But this is terrible.**
Social Worker:	**So, this is your third miscarriage. I know this great doctor who deals with problem pregnancies.**
Client:	**Oh, yeah, tell me about him.**
Social Worker:	**He's wonderful. He helped my sister with her pregnancy. You should go see him as soon as possible.**
Client:	**What's his phone number?**
Social Worker:	**Oh, I'll just set up your appointment right now because it's too stressful for you to worry about. You go home and rest.**

a)	What mistakes were made?

i.	**premature problem-solving**
ii.	**inappropriate self-disclosure**
iii.	**minimizing the problem**

b)	How might that response lead to barriers in furthering the relationship?

Client feels discounted, didn't explore feelings, doing "for" versus "with" the client.

c)	Corrected response: **You've suffered a great loss.**

CASE 1:

11-year-old female who is sharing for the first time that she has been sexually abused by her stepfather.

CL:	My stepfather. He touched me in places I know he is not supposed to touch. He told me that it was okay, but it doesn't feel okay.

SW:	I have to contact Child Protection Services right away.

CL:	No, please don't! He told me that he loves me. And we have done a couple of things that were a lot of fun together. He took me to a baseball game, and bought me ice cream. And took me to movies. He told me not to tell Mommy about it and he said that it was our secret.

SW:	Sharon, I'm really glad that you told me this secret. Lots of children are sexually abused. Sexual abuse is something that makes kids feel bad, like they've done something to deserve this. Now that I know, I have to contact the agency responsible for investigating sexual abuse.

CL:	You know, maybe I do things to make him touch me in that way.

SW:	You are not responsible for an adult's behavior. It's his problem. He needs help. No matter what, you are not to blame. Abusers try to put the responsibility on the child. It's wrong for him to do that. Wait here while I make the call.

a)	What mistakes were made?

i.
ii.
iii.

b)   How might that response lead to barriers in furthering the relationship?

c)   Your corrected response:

CASE 2:

A 54-year-old male whose job performance is slipping; he has some concerns about his future with the company.

CL: I've been this company's CEO for the past 25 years. I've been on top of the ladder for a long time, but I've seen a lot of things in the past year slipping. Dividends haven't been where they should be and, I don't know. People are starting to question me; I've started to question myself.

SW: So, you're starting to slack off on the job?

CL: Well, I wouldn't call it slacking off. I just don't have the drive for success that I use to have.

SW: It seems to me that maybe you don't care about your job. Maybe it's time for a change.

CL: I wouldn't say I don't care, but...

SW: You just said you are not doing the same quality on the job, no wonder you're in such a rut. What do you plan to do to change your situation?

a)   What mistakes were made?

i.
ii.
iii.

b)   How might that response lead to barriers in furthering the relationship?

c)   Your corrected response:

CASE 3:

A 22-year-old man who is in counseling at the insistence of his girlfriend and parents.

CL: It's my fourth year in college and my grades are not where they are supposed to be. My parents said they were going to cut me off financially if I didn't get my grades up. My girlfriend has been really getting on me, too, to do well in classes. Another thing I guess they think is contributing, is my drinking. I don't know if they are right or not.

SW: You know it is really important for you to do well in your classes if you want to get a job someday.

CL: Yeah I know.

SW: And you know it is wrong to drink because it causes problems with your girlfriend and with school, not to mention, multiple health problems down the road.

CL: Well, I guess that's true.

SW: How much do you drink each day?

CL: Maybe five or six beers a night, no more than my friends drink.

SW: Wow! Sounds like you're on your way to becoming an alcoholic.

a)   What mistakes were made?

i.
ii.
iii.

b)   How might that response lead to barriers in furthering the relationship?

c)   Your corrected response:

CASE 4:

A 30-year-old African American male who was severely injured in a recent accident.

CL: Yeah. I had this accident two weeks ago, driving my truck. I went right through the window. I'm probably going to lose my right leg.

SW: I'm sorry to hear that.

CL: Yeah. I'm sorry, too. Don't know if I can drive a truck without the use of my legs. The doctors say that with prosthetic and rehabilitation I'll be able to walk. I don't know how kindly I'll take to a fake leg.

SW: When will you know about the surgery?

CL: I'll know in a couple of days.

SW: If your leg is amputated, hopefully after a while, you'll get used to the idea. It takes time. Rehab can work wonders.

CL: If I lose my leg, I don't know if the firm will want me to keep driving. Maybe they have an office job for me, but I've never been real good at shuffling papers. Truck driving is basically all I've ever known.

SW: It's too early to worry about the worst, especially when no decision has been made yet. Have you always been so quick to jump to a bad conclusion?

CL: No, but there are bills to pay, you know. There's a whole family to support. This one truck accident and everything falls apart.

SW: But right now you don't know for sure how things will end up. Looking at all your strengths, I know you'll get through this. Plus, you'll be eligible for Workmen's Compensation, since this is a job-related injury.

CL: Yeah, but these are pretty rough times and there are hard days ahead of me. Truck driving is all I've really ever known.

SW: Let's get more information from the doctors, then we can move on to plan B.

a)   What mistakes were made?

i.
ii.
iii.

b)   How might that response lead to barriers in furthering the relationship?

c)   Your corrected response:

CASE 5:

A 14-year-old female was caught shoplifting.

CL: I got caught shoplifting yesterday. I went into the dressing room and put a shirt underneath my own shirt and the security guard caught me. Now they say they're going to press charges. It's a new department store policy. I'm 14, so they can't try me as an adult, which is a good thing. But obviously my mother is very angry with me.

SW: I know your mom is mad now, but I'm sure with time she'll get over it.

CL: Yeah, I guess so.

SW: Is this your first offense?

CL: Yeah.

SW: Then don't worry. They never prosecute first offenders harshly.

CL: Really?

SW: Sure, this whole thing will be over soon.

CL: Yeah, but my teachers know about it. They've been talking to me about it a lot. They make it seem like a bad situation.

SW: It sounds like the teachers are trying to scare you. I'm not saying it's okay to shoplift, but things will be fine. Remember, it's your first offense.

a)   What mistakes were made?

i.
ii.
iii.

b)   How might that response lead to barriers in furthering the relationship?

c)   Your corrected response:

CASE 6:

A 35-year-old Irish American woman who is frustrated with her neighbor.

CL: You know my next-door neighbor, Betty? We've been friends for a long time. But she is starting to test my patience, really.

SW: Go on.

CL: I'm home. I've got these three kids and I'm home all day. And, Betty, she just says to her daughter, "Why don't you go next door and play with Sue," my daughter. And her daughter comes over, which is fine. And the next thing I hear from Betty is that she's going out. She's gone, and I don't know where to find her. And her daughter is here with me for hours and hours at a time.

SW: Well, does her daughter cause problems with your three kids?

CL: No, my children enjoy having her over.

SW: Does she break things or roughhouse? Does she cry or complain about being at your place?

CL: No, she's really a good kid.

SW: Then it seems to me that you don't have a problem. I'm sure that you can work this out with Betty. In the meantime, be glad that your kids have a good friend.

CL: But, I want Betty to at least ask me rather than just sending Sue over.

SW: Your other alternative is to say something, but that may cause your friendship with Betty to end.

a)   What mistakes were made?

i.
ii.
iii.

b)   How might that response lead to barriers in furthering the relationship?

c)   Your corrected response:

CASE 7:

A 15-year-old girl who hates school. She recently hit her teacher.

CL: I hate these teachers. They're just pissing me off! Yesterday my English teacher wanted to keep me after school because I didn't do my homework. Screw her, you know? I got so mad I slapped her.

SW: So, you think your teacher is a punching bag?

CL: Yep! I know she is.

SW: Well, when I was in school, we had this teacher we called Miss Latrine because she smelled really bad.

CL: That's hilarious. We call my English teacher Big Nose for obvious reasons.

SW: Really, what other nicknames do you have?

a)   What mistakes were made?

i.
ii.
iii.

b)   How might that response lead to barriers in furthering the relationship?

c)   Your corrected response:

CASE 8:

A 36-year-old male who is frustrated with his parents' over-involvement in his life.

CL: It's my mother and father. They make me angry. They don't treat me like I'm 32; they treat me like I'm two. They want to know who my girlfriends are. They want to dictate where I work and where I live. They still want me to live at home, and I don't want to live at home. I want to live my own life.

SW: So here you are, an adult, and your parents treat you as though you can't make any decisions for yourself? Or if you do, they're wrong?

CL: That's right. And sometimes I screw up just to spite them, just to get them angry. I think I got fired from my last job just so I could see the look on their faces after I told them I got fired from this really good job. I don't know what they expect from me. It's like I'm not their little baby boy anymore. I'm a man, I'm an adult. I need to make mistakes and I need to do things on my own.

SW: So, what was the job you got fired from?

CL: Oh, I worked at an insurance company as a consultant.

SW: Did you find that to be a fulfilling job?

CL: Yeah, I guess. But weren't we talking about my relationship with my parents though?

SW: Yes we were, but I need to know a little more about you. Do you currently have a girlfriend?

CL: No, not now.

a)   What mistakes were made?

i.
ii.
iii.

b)   How might that response lead to barriers in furthering the relationship?

c)   Your corrected response:

CASE 9:

A 17- year-old African American female who is experiencing trouble at home, particularly with her stepfather.

SW: Juanita, you were talking about the difficulties you were having at home. The problems with your stepfather and that things were getting so bad that you decided to leave. Tell me what's been going on since the last time we met.

CL: I'm back at home, but my Stepdad doesn't even talk to me anymore. He's apparently really upset that I ran away from home. My mother, I guess, didn't really deal with it very well and was very upset. She cried all the time and couldn't eat. And he blames me for all that. He hates me more than he did before and won't even speak to me. So walking around our house is like, is like walking on eggshells and it's intolerable. I hate being there. None of this is my fault.

SW: Well, let's set some goals that you can work on in dealing with your stepfather.

CL: Okay, what kind of goals?

SW: Well, maybe you could try to start one conversation with him each day.

CL: I'm not sure I'm ready to do that.

SW: If you want things to improve, this is what I'd do. It's an important step for you.

CL: Well, I don't know.

SW: How about trying to say one nice thing to him between now and our next session? That will help open up communication.

a)   What mistakes were made?

i.
ii.
iii.

b)   How might that response lead to barriers in furthering the relationship?

c)   Your corrected response:

CASE 10:

A 20-year-old White female who was recently released from jail.

SW: Hi, Andrea, how have you been recently?

CL: Well, I've been okay since…

SW: So, that's nice. What is going on in your life now?

CL: I got out of jail about…

SW: You were in jail?

CL: Yeah, I was in jail for hitting my supervisor

SW: That's terrible. Why did you hit your supervisor? You knew you'd get in trouble.

CL: She set me off. It's just so hard to be a black wo…

SW: Keep going.

CL: To be a black woman in a white office.

SW: But that's always a reality in your life—you can't just punch someone out because you don't like her attitude. Did you get fired?

CL: No, but I've been resigned to another unit.

SW: Good. It's best to keep your opinions and hands to yourself so this doesn't happen again. Next time you could loose your job for good.

a)   What mistakes were made?

i.
ii.
iii.

b)   How might that response lead to barriers in furthering the relationship?

c)   Your corrected response:

CASE 11:

A 40-year-old female whose boyfriend recently broke up with her.

SW: Hi, Tiffany. How are you today?

CL: Fine. How are you?

SW: (silence)

CL: So, how are you?

SW: I'm okay. What brought you in today?

CL: Well, my boyfriend just broke up with me. It's been really hard to figure out if I want to date anyone else or just be single for a while. I'm getting older and starting to worry about my marriage prospects.

SW: (silence)

CL: And I don't know what to do.

SW: (silence)

CL: And I was wondering if you could help me.

SW: Oh...?

CL: See, I hate to be alone. I can't stand not having someone in my life.

SW: OK. What other problems do you have?

a)   What mistakes were made?

i.
ii.
iii.

b)   How might that response lead to barriers in furthering the relationship?

c)   Your corrected response:

CASE 12:

An 18-year-old female who is pregnant and searching for guidance.

SW: So how have you been doing, Jennifer?

CL: Well, okay, okay I guess. Actually, I'm not okay.

SW: What's been going on?

CL: I just found out yesterday that I'm pregnant, and I don't know what to do.

SW: Are you positive that you are pregnant?

CL: Yes, I am.

SW: Have you discussed it with your parents yet?

CL: No, I haven't. And I don't know if I should.

SW: Why not? It's really important that your parents know.

CL: I know it is, but it's just too hard.

SW: I realize that, but your parents can help you make decisions for you and the baby.

CL: I guess.

SW: So, you could tell them right now and ask them to come over and meet with us.

CL: Well, if you think that's best, I will.

SW: It is.

CL: What if they freak out?

SW: I'm sure they'll be upset, but honesty is always the best policy. How long do you think you can hide the pregnancy from them?

a)   What mistakes were made?

i.
ii.
iii.

b)   How might that response lead to barriers in furthering the relationship?

c)   Your corrected response:

CASE 13:

23-year-old Hispanic male who is trying to get through college.

SW: Hello. The last time we met, you were talking about your birthday coming up and turning 23. Sounds like that was a real struggle for you.

CL: Yeah. Well, I'm going to be 23 in December and all my friends have graduated. And I'm not quite there yet. Everybody looks at me and they're saying, "Oh, he's still in college. He's never going to get out. He's wasting his life."

SW: How do you see it?

CL: I feel badly about the whole thing. I transferred a lot, trying to find a decent major. And basically, I'm happy with social work. I'd like to get out sooner and start working so I can pay off all the loans that I have after the last six years of school.

SW: I'm sure that even if you have to stay in school longer, you will get your loans paid off.

CL: I don't know. I owe a lot of money.

SW: Most graduates owe a lot of money, but they make it.

CL: I guess most do, but I'm still scared.

SW: It's scary to owe a lot of money. I know. I had college loans too. It took me 10 years to pay them off, but I did and now things are fine. I'm proud of myself.

a)   What mistakes were made?

i.
ii.
iii.

b)   How might that response lead to barriers in furthering the relationship?

c)   Your corrected response:

CASE 14:

A 28-year-old female who is frustrated with the school's treatment of her daughter.

CL: You know this is the fifth time this week that the teacher has called about my daughter, and I'm fed up. I don't see what the big deal is. So what if my daughter is spreading paint all over the walls? It seems to me that this is a creative expression. She's having fun.

SW: I wonder whether Van Gogh's first-grade teacher complained to his mother.

CL: That's how I feel. That's exactly how I feel about it. This could be creativity in the making. This kid, she just loves having fun at school. She's not a troublemaker. The teachers don't call to say she's hitting other kids or fighting or anything like that. It's always in relationship to expressing herself through art. I have this child, this prodigy, and the teacher is squashing her creativity.

SW: So, today it's Walt Whitman Elementary School, tomorrow it's the Sistine Chapel.

CL: Well...I would say that.

SW: I'd call the teacher, set up an appointment to meet, and tell her exactly how you feel.

CL: I don't want her to get mad at me.

SW: Hey—this is your daughter here. You have to stand up for her.

a) What mistakes were made?

i.
i.
iii.

b) How might that response lead to barriers in furthering the relationship?

c) Your corrected response:

Putting it All Together

The exercises in this section of the workbook require you to use the skills you've learned in the previous sections.

Case 1

A 35-year-old Chinese American male. He is seeking help regarding suspected health problem. He believes the illness may be serious.

CL: I've been fainting at different times. It's scaring me. I don't know what I have. I don't know what's wrong. I don't know if it's something physical or if it's psychological.

SW: Right now you are extremely unsure about what might be going on with you physically and emotionally.

CL: Yes, plus I'm afraid of what to tell my family. It might be something serious. I don't know if it is something, like, genetic. This could be a very bad thing and I don't know how my family would react.

SW: Part of your concern is not just for your own health, but you are scared to tell your parents, you are afraid of their reaction.

CL: And, I guess I'm also afraid of my reaction. I suppose I should go to the doctor. It sounds serious, these fainting spells. I've looked in medical books, but I can't figure out what it is. And I'm afraid that if I go to a doctor she'll tell me it's serious. I don't know if I can take it.

SW: As you're trying to figure this out, you become more and more uncertain. "What is wrong with me? Is this something that is treatable?"

CL: I feel awful. I feel scared. And I just feel in my gut that this is a terrible situation.

SW: Summarization

Your response:

_____

_____

_____

Case 2

A 40-year-old female. She has just had a third miscarriage. She is seeking help in coping with her loss.

CL: This is just awful. Three miscarriages, and my husband and I really want a baby. And I just feel, I don't know, as if I'm paying for something that I've done before.

SW: These miscarriages have left you feeling so out of control.

CL: And I thought that after the first one that...the doctor told me that it would be all right for the next time. And then it happened again. And now it happened again...this is just screwy. I'm really depressed about it.

SW: It's a tremendous loss.

CL: I know. And after the second one, I thought that it was just not worth going through this again. I feel like this cloud is over me. I don't know what to do now. I feel hurt, and alone, and scared.

SW: Kelly, your feelings are very understandable. You suffered repeated trauma. You wanted a baby, and now it feels as though it may never happen.

CL: Why? I mean, I ask why? Nobody deserves to suffer. I'm a healthy person. I just don't understand why God is punishing me like this.

SW: You wonder, "I take good care of myself. I'm aware of my own body and the things I need to do to ensure healthy pregnancy. Now the bottom has fallen out, for the third time."

CL: I want a baby so badly, I just want to be a mom. I want to raise a child. And when I found out I was pregnant, it's like a roller coaster. Things were going so well and we, we were going to build a nursery, and then this happened.

SW: <u>Reflection of feeling</u>

Your response:

_____

_____

_____

Case 3

A 30-year-old Hispanic male. He is considering going back to school to become a physician. His family obligations and self-doubt contribute to his dilemma.

CL: Thirty years old. The big 3 – 0. When I was in my early twenties I wanted to go to college, but I couldn't. I didn't have the money. My father was sick and I had to work to pay the bills. Now I can afford to go to college, but I'm not 20 anymore. I want to be a doctor, but medical school at 30?

SW: When you think about it, it's really exciting: the possibility of a new career, going back to school. But it's challenging. There's a lot of work involved. It is a huge decision.

CL: The thought of hitting those books, long hours studying—I don't know. It's tailor-made for the young. I know I want it. I always wanted to be a doctor. It's just now that I have the opportunity.

SW: Now, the opportunity is there, but so is your sense of doubt.

CL: Right. Medical school is difficult. It is an uphill battle: lab work, classroom time, a lot of memorization. You know, now I'm married, I want time with my wife. I don't know what to do.

SW: Part of what I'm hearing is that you really want to do this. But to take this on at 30 with a family, with other responsibilities, poses a real challenge.

CL: Yeah. Being a doctor has always been my life's ambition. But there's a lot of sacrifice, a lot of commitment to achieve this goal.

What issues would you want to discuss the next time you meet? (List 3)

_____

_____

_____

Your response:

_____

_____

_____

Case 4

A 30-year-old female who is fed up with her ex-husband. He continues to break his promises.

CL: You know, we've talked about my ex. He's an absolute jerk. We have three kids. John said he wanted kids, marriage, the whole thing. Now he's dumped me, he's out of the picture. We never see him anymore and I'm broke. He said he'd be involved in our lives and now he's gone. And it really makes me mad that he made this promise to me about our kids. I don't even care about me. It's our kids. And I can hardly afford to pay the rent and now he's gone.

SW: John has left you with all the responsibility and you're furious with him.

CL: Yes. If he cared about our kids, like he said he did, he would cough up the child support. But you know what? I haven't heard from him in four months, not a dime. I just can't believe he's doing this to us.

SW: <u>Reflection of feeling</u>

Your response:

_____

_____

Case 5

A 45-year-old female. She is currently in an emotionally and physically abusive relationship.

CL: You know, I really love my partner, I love Elaine a lot. But this stuff has to stop.

SW: I know last week, we were discussing the violence that has been going on between you and Elaine.

CL: Yeah. She got so mad at me. And, no matter how much I try to make her understand, she just doesn't listen. And you know I tried talking to her, like you suggested, and you know what? It got me into bigger trouble.

SW: What do you mean by bigger trouble?

CL: She told me that the social worker is feeding me garbage. She thinks that I should do what she says. She thinks that no matter what I want to do it doesn't count. And you've been telling me that it's important to know how I feel and know what I want. And when I tell her what I want, she hits me.

SW: <u>Paraphrasing</u>

Your response:

_____

_____

Case 6

A 35-year-old male. He is afraid of making a permanent commitment to his girlfriend. He wants things to remain "open," but is afraid of losing her.

SW: Antonio, the last time we met, you were talking about your girlfriend. You really love her but recently you have been feeling pressure from her to get married.

CL: Right. We have been together for seven years now, which is a long time. The relationship has gotten very comfortable, it's almost like putting socks on, very natural. We both understand each other. We're very open with each and know each other, pretty much inside and out. I guess the next step is to get married, and that is what she really wants. Her family is very traditional. And you know we live together and have been for four years now. I'm fine with just living with each other. I don't need a piece of paper. She wants it to be official.

SW: If you had your choice, it would be to keep things as they are.

CL: Yes! Things are fine, you know? If it's not broken, don't fix it. I always thought that things were going fine. She is even thinking of having a child, which is okay with me. But she wants to go through the formalities. My parents are divorced and everyone who's married seems to be very unhappy. And I don't know if I want that.

SW: Interpretation

Your response:

_____

_____

_____

Case 7

A 28-year-old Native American who is unemployed. He wants to remain on the reservation, but has been unable to find a job.

CL: The electric company turned off the power. I think this is final, it's the last straw. I've been unemployed for three months and delinquent on all my bills. I don't know what to do about this.

SW: That's a lot to handle right now. Did this just happen?

CL: Yeah. I've been out of a job for three months, laid off, you know. Working in an auto shop--I've been working there for 15 years, you know, living from paycheck to paycheck, but still making it. What they give you on unemployment can't even pay for necessities like electricity. So they turned it off.

SW: Now you're unsure where to turn, what to do.

CL: Yeah. Jobs sure aren't falling like leaves. I mean they're hard to find. I was born on the reservation; I grew up on the reservation. I don't want to leave. But it's looking like I'm going to have to leave. There's just no work. Plus, my wife is mad. We were married five years ago. We didn't expect this situation. I guess nobody does. Her family lives on the reservation, too. She doesn't want to leave, but we're going to have to leave. Got to find work in the city.

SW: <u>Reflection of feeling and open- ended question</u>

Your response:

_____

_____

_____

Case 8

A 35-year-old female who is waiting for her mammogram results. She is certain that cancer was found.

CL: They got the results of my tests. I went in for a mammogram. I knew it wasn't good news when the doctor called me and told me that he wanted to see me. Usually they just send a piece of paper saying your test results came back and everything's fine. This time I got a call, and I have to go in. It sounds like they found a lump on my breast.

SW: How are you feeling about this?

CL: Really scared. I've always kind of known that I was at high risk for breast cancer. My mom had breast cancer; her sister had breast cancer. Here I am, the third in the line. I'm sure it's cancer.

SW: What frightening news.

CL: I know. I hate having mammograms. In fact, I have avoided them. I figure if I don't know, at least then I don't have to deal with it. I knew I had to go in for this mammogram. It's been about two years since I've been in and that also scares me because if the cancer has been there for that long, who knows.

SW: <u>Reflection of feeling</u>

Your response:

_____

_____

_____

Case 9

A 15-year-old girl who is discussing her unexpected pregnancy.

SW: The last time we met you were trying to decide what to do about your pregnancy.

CL: Things are no better. My parents want me to have an abortion. I just don't feel I can do that. My boyfriend's parents want that, too. And Todd wants that. Everybody wants me to have an abortion and I'm feeling a lot of pressure.

SW: Everybody's saying having an abortion, get on with your life?

CL: Yeah, they just think that having a baby is going to ruin my life. And I realize that it's going to be difficult and it's going to be hard. But I just don't know if I can live with the fact that I killed my own baby.

SW: <u>Closed-ended question</u>

Your response:

_____

_____

Case 10

A 50-year-old African American male struggling with job-related issues.

CL: You know my job is really getting me down. I used to like going to work. I had lots of friends there, but now, I don't know, it's such a drag.

SW: When you say a "drag," what does that mean exactly?

CL: I don't know. I was promoted last year because I did a good job on a project. I got lots of praise. After the job change I never quite got used to all the things I need to do. Mostly, it's supervising people. I used to be their friends, now I'm kind of the boss.

SW: You wonder if all this was worth the promotion?

CL: Definitely! I wish I could go back to being "one of the guys." I just don't like any part of what I'm doing.

SW: <u>Paraphrase</u>

Your response:

_____

Case 11

CL: It's my fourth year in college and my grades are not where they are supposed to be. My parents said that they were going to cut me off financially if I didn't get my grades up. My girlfriend has been really getting on me too. Another thing is, they think that I drink too much. I mean, I only drink at parties and all my friends are there. Drinking is part of college life, I thought.

SW: Evan, how do you see it?

CL: I'm not sure. I don't see myself drinking any more than my friends. There are probably 10 other friends of mine who should be in here before me. But my parents keep yelling in my ear. It's all they talk about.

SW: So, maybe you're at the point of questioning whether your drinking is contributing to your grades slipping.

CL: Yeah. But I just don't see it as a problem. I get up in the morning. Most of the time I make it to classes. I think every college student is an alcoholic, if that's the description.

SW: <u>Confrontation</u>

Your response:

Case 12

A 25-year-old female, struggling with issues related to her ex-boyfriend. He recently got married, which has left her hurt and confused.

CL: I just found out that Andy, the guy I dated for four years, got married.

SW: That's a shock?

CL: It really was.

SW: Did you have any idea?

CL: I knew that they had been together. But I didn't think they would get married.

SW: How are you feeling about it all?

CL: I can't sleep. I can't eat…and to top it off, he's having a reception in my hometown and inviting all my friends.

SW: It's like he's rubbing this in your face?

CL: That's his main goal; get married and hurt me.

SW: You really sound shaken by all of this. What led up to the break up?

CL: I can't even explain what happened. We had broken up a hundred times before. He was evil; he was seriously an evil person. I just gave so much to him; and finally I felt like I couldn't give anymore. But I expected him to come back to me.

SW: You gave this relationship your all. You put up with a lot from him and then he leaves and married someone else.

CL: Yeah, after knowing her for six months.

SW: Was your hope that eventually you two would get married?

CL: Honestly no. It was that he would want me back, and I'd be able to say "no." I've been so weak with him, unbelievably weak. He would cheat on me and come back to me, and I'd take him back. This time, I wanted to hear, "Cheryl take me back," and I'd be able to say, "No way."

SW: You wanted the satisfaction of saying to him, "I'm strong enough now. You're out of my life." And he didn't give you that opportunity?

CL: He had the nerve to bring her over to my house so we could meet. What kind of person is he? What kind of person am I to have put up with all of this crap?

SW: Interpretation

Your response:

_____

_____

Case 12, Continued

SW: How were you able to end the relationship with him?

CL: It was kind of a fluke. It was New Year's Eve. We had been partying together. We met some people. Next thing I know, Andy's with this girl. Later he came to my house. He wanted the money I owed him. I gave it to him and slammed the door. That was it.

SW: That was the last straw. You said that you were really weak in the relationship, that you put up with years of abuse. Tell me more about that.

CL: Well, when I was in college, I was in counseling trying to resolve my relationship with him. To do things that were stronger. But every week I would go there, and my social worker wanted to strangle me. I'd come in there, "Oh we got back together" or "Oh we broke up." She never said I was stupid, but I was. I stopped counseling because I wasn't ready to end my relationship with Andy. And now I can't understand why he is so happy and I'm not. I'm sick of it. How dare he be happy?

SW: <u>Summarization</u>

Your response:

_____

_____

_____

Case 12, Continued

SW: You're questioning, "What is it about me that I stayed in the relationship for so long?"

CL: "What's wrong with the way I look?" "Or am I not fun?" I gave him everything. I know I have low self-esteem—I can admit that. The four years that I was with him, I did nothing but be there for him. I took all kinds of abuse. There is nothing positive about me.

SW: It's hard for you to see your strengths?

CL: Yep! It's always been that way.

SW: <u>Open-ended question</u>

Your response:

_____

_____

_____

Case 12, Continued

SW: Cheryl, you said that your family has always been a source of strength for you, that they rallied behind you after you told them about Andy's marriage. They knew you'd be devastated.

CL: My family is great. I mean, they definitely didn't like him. And they're glad it's not me he married. They stuck by me and helped me. Deep down I'm sure they are disappointed in me. That I stayed with him for so long.

SW: <u>Clarification</u>

Your response:

_____

_____

_____

Case 12, Continued

SW: You said that you see yourself as a very caring and giving person. In some ways, that also may have caused the trouble with Andy. You're always giving and wanting to take care of him.

CL: Oh yeah, definitely.

SW: Because he expected it, too?

CL: I'm just like my mom.

SW: You think you're just like your mom. What's she like?

CL: She's very caring. She would do anything for anybody, especially her children. She's a wonderful person. She and my dad have a great marriage. That's probably why they were so upset with me. They make it look so easy. Why can't it be that way for me too?

SW: <u>Information giving</u>

Your response:

_____

_____

_____

National Association of Social Workers

CODE OF ETHICS

Effective January 1, 1997

Preamble

The primary mission of the social work profession is to enhance human well-being and help meet the basic human needs of all people, with particular attention to the needs and empowerment of people who are vulnerable, oppressed, and living in poverty. A historic and defining feature of social work is the profession's focus on individual well-being in a social context and the well-being of society. Fundamental to social work is attention to the environmental forces that create, contribute to, and address problems in living.

Social workers promote social justice and social change with and on behalf of clients. "Clients" is used inclusively to refer to individuals, families, groups, organizations, and communities. Social workers are sensitive to cultural and ethnic diversity and strive to end discrimination, oppression, poverty, and other forms of social injustice. These activities may be in the form of direct practice, community organizing, supervision, consultation, administration, advocacy, social and political action, policy development and implementation, education, and research and evaluation. Social workers seek to enhance the capacity of people to address their own needs. Social workers also seek to promote the responsiveness of organizations, communities, and other social institutions to individuals' needs and social problems.

The mission of the social work profession is rooted in a set of core values. These core values, embraced by social workers throughout the profession's history, are the foundation of social work's unique purpose and perspective:

- service
- social justice
- dignity and worth of the person
- importance of human relationships
- integrity
- competence.

This constellation of core values reflects what is unique to the social work profession. Core values, and the principles that flow from them, must be balanced within the context and complexity of the human experience.

Purpose of the NASW Code of Ethics

Professional ethics are at the core of social work. The profession has an obligation to articulate its basic values, ethical principles, and ethical standards. The *NASW Code of Ethics* sets forth these values, principles, and standards to guide social workers' conduct.

The *Code* is relevant to all social workers and social work students, regardless of their professional functions, the settings in which they work, or the populations they serve.

The *NASW Code of Ethics* serves six purposes:

1. The *Code* identifies core values on which social work's mission is based.
2. The *Code* summarizes broad ethical principles that reflect the profession's core values and establishes a set of specific ethical standards that should be used to guide social work practice.
3. The *Code* is designed to help social workers identify relevant considerations when professional obligations conflict or ethical uncertainties arise.
4. The *Code* provides ethical standards to which the general public can hold the social work profession accountable.
5. The *Code* socializes practitioners new to the field to social work's mission, values, ethical principles, and ethical standards.
6. The *Code* articulates standards that the social work profession itself can use to assess whether social workers have engaged in unethical conduct. NASW has formal procedures to adjudicate ethics complaints filed against its members.[1] In subscribing to this *Code*, social workers are required to cooperate in its implementation, participate in NASW adjudication proceedings, and abide by any NASW disciplinary rulings or sanctions based on it.

[1] For information on NASW adjudication procedures, see *NASW Procedures for the Adjudication of Grievances*.

The *Code* offers a set of values, principles, and standards to guide decision making and conduct when ethical issues arise. It does not provide a set of rules that prescribe how social workers should act in all situations. Specific applications of the *Code* must take into account the context in which it is being considered and the possibility of conflicts among the *Code*'s values, principles, and standards. Ethical responsibilities flow from all human relationships, from the personal and familial to the social and professional.

Further, the *NASW Code of Ethics* does not specify which values, principles, and standards are most important and ought to outweigh others in instances when they conflict. Reasonable differences of opinion can and do exist among social workers with respect to the ways in which values, ethical principles, and ethical standards should be rank ordered when they conflict. Ethical decision making in a given situation must apply the informed judgment of the individual social worker and should also consider how the issues would be judged in a peer review process where the ethical standards of the profession would be applied.

Ethical decision making is a process. There are many instances in social work where simple answers are not available to resolve complex ethical issues. Social workers should take into consideration all the values, principles, and standards in this *Code* that are relevant to any situation in which ethical judgment is warranted. Social workers' decisions and actions should be consistent with the spirit as well as the letter of this *Code*.

In addition to this *Code*, there are many other sources of information about ethical thinking that may be useful. Social workers should consider ethical theory and principles generally, social work theory and research, laws, regulations, agency policies, and other relevant codes of ethics, recognizing that among codes of ethics social workers should consider the *NASW Code of Ethics* as their primary source. Social workers also should be aware of the impact on ethical decision making of their clients' and their own personal values and cultural and religious beliefs and practices. They should be aware of any conflicts between personal and professional values and deal with them responsibly. For additional guidance social workers should consult the relevant literature on professional ethics and ethical decision making and seek appropriate consultation when faced with ethical dilemmas. This may involve consultation with an agency-based or social work organization's ethics committee, a regulatory body, knowledgeable colleagues, supervisors, or legal counsel.

Instances may arise when social workers' ethical obligations conflict with agency policies or relevant laws or regulations. When such conflicts occur, social workers must make a responsible effort to resolve the conflict in a manner that is consistent with the values, principles, and standards expressed in this *Code*. If a reasonable resolution of the conflict does not appear possible, social workers should seek proper consultation before making a decision.

The *NASW Code of Ethics* is to be used by NASW and by individuals, agencies, organizations, and bodies (such as licensing and regulatory boards, professional liability insurance providers, courts of law, agency boards of directors, government agencies, and other professional groups) that choose to adopt it or use it as a frame of reference. Violation of standards in this *Code* does not automatically imply legal liability or violation of the law. Such determination can only be made in the context of legal and judicial proceedings. Alleged violations of the *Code* would be subject to a peer review process. Such processes are generally separate from legal or administrative procedures and insulated from legal review or proceedings to allow the profession to counsel and discipline its own members.

A code of ethics cannot guarantee ethical behavior. Moreover, a code of ethics cannot resolve all ethical issues or disputes or capture the richness and complexity involved in striving to make responsible choices within a moral community. Rather, a code of ethics sets forth values, ethical principles, and ethical standards to which professionals aspire and by which their actions can be judged. Social workers' ethical behavior should result from their personal commitment to engage in ethical practice. The *NASW Code of Ethics* reflects the commitment of all social workers to uphold the profession's values and to act ethically. Principles and standards must be applied by individuals of good char-acter who discern moral questions and, in good faith, seek to make reliable ethical judgments.

Ethical Principles

The following broad ethical principles are based on social work's core values of service, social justice, dignity and worth of the person, importance of human relationships, integrity, and competence. These principles set forth ideals to which all social workers should aspire.

Value: *Service*

Ethical Principle: *Social workers' primary goal is to help people in need and to address social problems.*

Social workers elevate service to others above self-interest. Social workers draw on their knowledge, values, and skills to help people in need and to address social problems. Social workers are encouraged to volunteer some portion of their professional skills with no expectation of significant financial return (pro bono service).

Value: *Social Justice*

Ethical Principle: *Social workers challenge social injustice.*

Social workers pursue social change, particularly with and on behalf of vulnerable and oppressed individuals and groups of people. Social workers' social change efforts are focused primarily on issues of poverty, unemployment, discrimination, and other forms of social injustice. These activities seek to promote sensitivity to and knowledge about oppression and cultural and ethnic diversity. Social workers strive to ensure access to needed information, services, and resources; equality of opportunity; and meaningful participation in decision making for all people.

Value: *Dignity and Worth of the Person*

Ethical Principle: *Social workers respect the inherent dignity and worth of the person.*

Social workers treat each person in a caring and respectful fashion, mindful of individual differences and cultural and ethnic diversity. Social workers promote clients' socially responsible self-determination. Social workers seek to enhance clients' capacity and opportunity to change and to address their own needs. Social workers are cognizant of their dual responsibility to clients and to the broader society. They seek to resolve conflicts between clients' interests and the broader society's interests in a socially responsible manner consistent with the values, ethical principles, and ethical standards of the profession.

Value: *Importance of Human Relationships*

Ethical Principle: *Social workers recognize the central importance of human relationships.*

Social workers understand that relationships between and among people are an important vehicle for change. Social workers engage people as partners in the helping process. Social workers seek to strengthen relationships among people in a purposeful effort to promote, restore, maintain, and enhance the well-being of individuals, families, social groups, organizations, and communities.

Value: *Integrity*

Ethical Principle: *Social workers behave in a trustworthy manner.*

Social workers are continually aware of the profession's mission, values, ethical principles, and ethical standards and practice in a manner consistent with them. Social workers act honestly and responsibly and promote ethical practices on the part of the organizations with which they are affiliated.

Value: *Competence*

Ethical Principle: *Social workers practice within their areas of competence and develop and enhance their professional expertise.*

Social workers continually strive to increase their professional knowledge and skills and to apply them in practice. Social workers should aspire to contribute to the knowledge base of the profession.

Ethical Standards

The following ethical standards are relevant to the professional activities of all social workers. These standards concern (1) social workers' ethical responsibilities to clients, (2) social workers' ethical responsibilities to colleagues, (3) social workers' ethical responsibilities in practice settings, (4) social workers' ethical responsibilities as professionals, (5) social workers' ethical responsibilities to the social work profession, and (6) social workers' ethical responsibilities to the broader society.

Some of the standards that follow are enforceable guidelines for professional conduct, and some are aspirational. The extent to which each standard is enforceable is a matter of professional judgment to be exercised by those responsible for reviewing alleged violations of ethical standards.

1. SOCIAL WORKERS' ETHICAL RESPONSIBILITIES TO CLIENTS

1.01 Commitment to Clients

Social workers' primary responsibility is to promote the well-being of clients. In general, clients' interests are primary. However, social workers' responsibility to the larger society or specific legal obligations may on limited occasions supersede the loyalty owed clients, and clients should be so advised. (Examples include when a social worker is required by law to report that a client has abused a child or has threatened to harm self or others.)

1.02 Self-Determination

Social workers respect and promote the right of clients to self-determination and assist clients in their efforts to identify and clarify their goals. Social workers may limit clients' right to self-determination when, in the social workers' professional judgment, clients' actions or potential actions pose a serious, foreseeable, and imminent risk to themselves or others.

1.03 Informed Consent

(a) Social workers should provide services to clients only in the context of a professional relationship based, when appropriate, on valid informed consent. Social workers should use clear and understandable language to inform clients of the purpose of the services, risks related to the services, limits to services because of the requirements of a third-party payer, relevant costs, reasonable alternatives, clients' right to refuse or withdraw consent, and the time frame covered by the consent. Social workers should provide clients with an opportunity to ask questions.

(b) In instances when clients are not literate or have difficulty understanding the primary language used in the practice setting, social workers should take steps to ensure clients' comprehension. This may include providing clients with a detailed verbal explanation or arranging for a qualified interpreter or translator whenever possible.

(c) In instances when clients lack the capacity to provide informed consent, social workers should protect clients' interests by seeking permission from an appropriate third party, informing clients consistent with the clients' level of understanding. In such instances social workers should seek to ensure that the third party acts in a manner consistent with clients' wishes and interests. Social workers should take reasonable steps to enhance such clients' ability to give informed consent.

(d) In instances when clients are receiving services involuntarily, social workers should provide information about the nature and extent of services and about the extent of clients' right to refuse service.

(e) Social workers who provide services via electronic media (such as computer, telephone, radio, and television) should inform recipients of the limitations and risks associated with such services.

(f) Social workers should obtain clients' informed consent before audiotaping or videotaping clients or permitting observation of services to clients by a third party.

1.04 Competence

(a) Social workers should provide services and represent themselves as competent only within the boundaries of their education, training, license, certification, consultation received, supervised experience, or other relevant professional experience.

(b) Social workers should provide services in substantive areas or use intervention techniques or approaches that are new to them only after engaging in appropriate study, training, consultation, and supervision from people who are competent in those interventions or techniques.

(c) When generally recognized standards do not exist with respect to an emerging area of practice, social workers should exercise careful judgment and take responsible steps (including appropriate education, research, training, consultation, and supervision) to ensure the competence of their work and to protect clients from harm.

1.05 Cultural Competence and Social Diversity

(a) Social workers should understand culture and its function in human behavior and society, recognizing the strengths that exist in all cultures.

(b) Social workers should have a knowledge base of their clients' cultures and be able to demonstrate competence in the provision of services that are sensitive to clients' cultures and to differences among people and cultural groups.

(c) Social workers should obtain education about and seek to understand the nature of social diversity and oppression with respect to race, ethnicity, national origin, color, sex, sexual orientation, age, marital status, political belief, religion, and mental or physical disability.

1.06 Conflicts of Interest

(a) Social workers should be alert to and avoid conflicts of interest that interfere with the exercise of professional discretion and impartial judgment. Social workers should inform clients when a real or potential conflict of interest arises and take reasonable steps to resolve the issue in a manner that makes the clients' interests primary and protects clients' interests to the greatest extent possible. In some cases, protecting clients' interests may require termination of the professional relationship with proper referral of the client.

(b) Social workers should not take unfair advantage of any professional relationship or exploit others to further their personal, religious, political, or business interests.

(c) Social workers should not engage in dual or multiple relationships with clients or former clients in which there is a risk of exploitation or potential harm to the client. In instances when dual or multiple relationships are unavoidable, social workers should take steps to protect clients and are responsible for setting clear, appropriate, and culturally sensitive boundaries. (Dual or multiple relationships occur when social workers relate to clients in more than one relationship, whether professional, social, or business. Dual or multiple relationships can occur simultaneously or consecutively.)

(d) When social workers provide services to two or more people who have a relationship with each other (for example, couples, family members), social workers should clarify with all parties which individuals will be considered clients and the nature of social workers' professional obligations to the various individuals who are receiving services. Social workers who anticipate a conflict of interest among the individuals receiving services or who anticipate having to perform in potentially conflicting roles (for example, when a social worker is asked to testify in a child custody dispute or divorce proceedings involving clients) should clarify their role with the parties involved and take appropriate action to minimize any conflict of interest.

1.07 Privacy and Confidentiality

(a) Social workers should respect clients' right to privacy. Social workers should not solicit private information from clients unless it is essential to providing services or conducting social work evaluation or research. Once private information is shared, standards of confidentiality apply.

(b) Social workers may disclose confidential information when appropriate with valid consent from a client or a person legally authorized to consent on behalf of a client.

(c) Social workers should protect the confidentiality of all information obtained in the course of professional service, except for compelling professional reasons. The general expectation that social workers will keep information confidential does not apply when disclosure is necessary to prevent serious, foreseeable, and imminent harm to a client or other identifiable person or when laws or regulations require disclosure without a client's consent. In all instances, social workers should disclose the least amount of confidential information necessary to achieve the desired purpose; only information that is directly relevant to the purpose for which the disclosure is made should be revealed.

(d) Social workers should inform clients, to the extent possible, about the disclosure of confidential information and the potential consequences, when feasible before the disclosure is made. This applies whether social workers disclose confidential information on the basis of a legal requirement or client consent.

(e) Social workers should discuss with clients and other interested parties the nature of confidentiality and limitations of clients' right to confidentiality. Social workers should review with clients circumstances where confidential information may be requested and where disclosure of confidential information may be legally required. This discussion should occur as soon as possible in the social worker–client relationship and as needed throughout the course of the relationship.

(f) When social workers provide counseling services to families, couples, or groups, social workers should seek agreement among the parties involved concerning each individual's right to
confidentiality and obligation to preserve the confidentiality
of information shared by others. Social workers should inform participants in family, couples, or group counseling that social workers cannot guarantee that all participants will honor such agreements.

(g) Social workers should inform clients involved in family, couples, marital, or group counseling of the social worker's, employer's, and agency's policy concerning the social worker's disclosure of confidential information among the parties involved in the counseling.

(h) Social workers should not disclose confidential information to third-party payers unless clients have authorized such
disclosure.

(i) Social workers should not discuss confidential information in any setting unless privacy can be ensured. Social workers should not discuss confidential information in public or semipublic areas such as hallways, waiting rooms, elevators, and restaurants.

(j) Social workers should protect the confidentiality of clients during legal proceedings to the extent permitted by law. When a court of law or other legally authorized body orders social workers to disclose confidential or privileged information without a client's consent and such disclosure could cause harm to the client, social workers should request that the court withdraw the order or limit the order as narrowly as possible or maintain the records under seal, unavailable for public inspection.

(k) Social workers should protect the confidentiality of clients when responding to requests from members of the media.

(l) Social workers should protect the confidentiality of clients' written and electronic records and other sensitive information. Social workers should take reasonable steps to ensure that clients' records are stored in a secure location and that clients' records are not available to others who are not authorized to have access.

(m) Social workers should take precautions to ensure and maintain the confidentiality of information transmitted to other parties through the use of computers, electronic mail, facsimile machines, telephones and telephone answering machines, and other electronic or computer technology. Disclosure of identifying information should be avoided whenever possible.

(n) Social workers should transfer or dispose of clients' records in a manner that protects clients' confidentiality and is consistent with state statutes governing records and social work licensure.

(o) Social workers should take reasonable precautions to protect client confidentiality in the event of the social worker's termination of practice, incapacitation, or death.

(p) Social workers should not disclose identifying information when discussing clients for teaching or training purposes unless the client has consented to disclosure of confidential information.

(q) Social workers should not disclose identifying information when discussing clients with consultants unless the client has consented to disclosure of confidential information or there is a compelling need for such disclosure.

(r) Social workers should protect the confidentiality of deceased clients consistent with the preceding standards.

1.08 Access to Records

(a) Social workers should provide clients with reasonable access to records concerning the clients. Social workers who are concerned that clients' access to their records could cause serious misunderstanding or harm to the client should provide assistance in interpreting the records and consultation with the client regarding the records. Social workers should limit clients' access to their records, or portions of their records, only in exceptional circumstances when there is compelling evidence that such access would cause serious harm to the client. Both clients' requests and the rationale for withholding some or all of the record should be documented in clients' files.

(b) When providing clients with access to their records, social workers should take steps to protect the confidentiality of other individuals identified or discussed in such records.

1.09 Sexual Relationships

(a) Social workers should under no circumstances engage in sexual activities or sexual contact with current clients, whether such contact is consensual or forced.

(b) Social workers should not engage in sexual activities or sexual contact with clients' relatives or other individuals with whom clients maintain a close personal relationship when there is a risk of exploitation or potential harm to the client. Sexual activity or sexual contact with clients' relatives or other individuals with whom clients maintain a personal relationship has the potential to be harmful to the client and may make it difficult for the social worker and client to maintain appropriate professional boundaries. Social workers—not their clients, their clients' relatives, or other individuals with whom the client maintains a personal relationship—assume the full burden for setting clear, appropriate, and culturally sensitive boundaries.

(c) Social workers should not engage in sexual activities or sexual contact with former clients because of the potential for harm to the client. If social workers engage in conduct contrary to this prohibition or claim that an exception to this prohibition is warranted because of extraordinary circumstances, it is social workers—not their clients—who assume the full burden of demonstrating that the former client has not been exploited, coerced, or manipulated, intentionally or unintentionally.

(d) Social workers should not provide clinical services to individuals with whom they have had a prior sexual relationship. Providing clinical services to a former sexual partner has the potential to be harmful to the individual and is likely to make it difficult for the social worker and individual to maintain appropriate professional boundaries.

1.10 Physical Contact

Social workers should not engage in physical contact with clients when there is a possibility of psychological harm to the client as a result of the contact (such as cradling or caressing clients). Social workers who engage in appropriate physical contact with clients are responsible for setting clear, appropriate, and culturally sensitive boundaries that govern such physical contact.

1.11 Sexual Harassment

Social workers should not sexually harass clients. Sexual harassment includes sexual advances, sexual solicitation, requests for sex-
usual favors, and other verbal or physical conduct of a sexual nature.

1.12 Derogatory Language

Social workers should not use derogatory language in their written or verbal communications to or about clients. Social workers should use accurate and respectful language in all communications to and about clients.

1.13 Payment for Services

(a) When setting fees, social workers should ensure that the fees are fair, reasonable, and commensurate with the services performed. Consideration should be given to clients' ability to pay.

(b) Social workers should avoid accepting goods or services from clients as payment for professional services. Bartering arrangements, particularly involving services, create the potential for conflicts of interest, exploitation, and inappropriate boundaries in social workers' relationships with clients. Social workers should explore and may participate in bartering only in very limited circumstances when it can be demonstrated that such arrangements are an accepted practice among professionals in the local community, considered to be essential for the provision of services, negotiated without coercion, and entered into at the client's initiative and with the client's informed consent. Social workers who accept goods or services from clients as payment for professional services assume the full burden of demonstrating that this arrangement will not be detrimental to the client or the professional relationship.

(c) Social workers should not solicit a private fee or other remuneration for providing services to clients who are entitled to such available services through the social workers' employer or agency.

1.14 Clients Who Lack Decision-Making Capacity

When social workers act on behalf of clients who lack the capacity to make informed decisions, social workers should take reasonable steps to safeguard the interests and rights of those clients.

1.15 Interruption of Services

Social workers should make reasonable efforts to ensure continuity of services in the event that services are interrupted by factors such as unavailability, relocation, illness, disability, or death.

1.16 Termination of Services

(a) Social workers should terminate services to clients and professional relationships with them when such services and relationships are no longer required or no longer serve the clients' needs or interests.

(b) Social workers should take reasonable steps to avoid abandoning clients who are still in need of services. Social workers should withdraw services precipitously only under unusual circumstances, giving careful consideration to all factors in the situation and taking care to minimize possible adverse effects. Social workers should assist in making appropriate arrangements for continuation of services when necessary.

(c) Social workers in fee-for-service settings may terminate services to clients who are not paying an overdue balance if the financial contractual arrangements have been made clear to the client, if the client does not pose an imminent danger to self or others, and if the clinical and other consequences of the current nonpayment have been addressed and discussed with the client.

(d) Social workers should not terminate services to pursue a social, financial, or sexual relationship with a client.

(e) Social workers who anticipate the termination or interruption of services to clients should notify clients promptly and seek the transfer, referral, or continuation of services in relation to the clients' needs and preferences.

(f) Social workers who are leaving an employment setting should inform clients of appropriate options for the continuation of services and of the benefits and risks of the options.

2. SOCIAL WORKERS' ETHICAL RESPONSIBILITIES TO COLLEAGUES

2.01 Respect

(a) Social workers should treat colleagues with respect and should represent accurately and fairly the qualifications, views, and obligations of colleagues.

(b) Social workers should avoid unwarranted negative criticism of colleagues in communications with clients or with other professionals. Unwarranted negative criticism may include demeaning comments that refer to colleagues' level of competence or to individuals' attributes such as race, ethnicity, national origin, color, sex, sexual orientation, age, marital status, political belief, religion, and mental or physical disability.

(c) Social workers should cooperate with social work colleagues and with colleagues of other professions when such cooperation serves the well-being of clients.

2.02 Confidentiality

Social workers should respect confidential information shared by colleagues in the course of their professional relationships and transactions. Social workers should ensure that such colleagues understand social workers' obligation to respect confidentiality and any exceptions related to it.

2.03 Interdisciplinary Collaboration

(a) Social workers who are members of an interdisciplinary team should participate in and contribute to decisions that affect the well-being of clients by drawing on the perspectives, values, and experiences of the social work profession. Professional and ethical obligations of the interdisciplinary team as a whole and of its individual members should be clearly established.

(b) Social workers for whom a team decision raises ethical concerns should attempt to resolve the disagreement through appropriate channels. If the disagreement cannot be resolved, social workers should pursue other avenues to address their concerns consistent with client well-being.

2.04 Disputes Involving Colleagues

(a) Social workers should not take advantage of a dispute between a colleague and an employer to obtain a position or otherwise advance the social workers' own interests.

(b) Social workers should not exploit clients in disputes with colleagues or engage clients in any inappropriate discussion of conflicts between social workers and their colleagues.

2.05 Consultation

(a) Social workers should seek the advice and counsel of colleagues whenever such consultation is in the best interests of clients.

(b) Social workers should keep themselves informed about colleagues' areas of expertise and competencies. Social workers should seek consultation only from colleagues who have demonstrated knowledge, expertise, and competence related to the subject of the consultation.

(c) When consulting with colleagues about clients, social workers should disclose the least amount of information necessary to achieve the purposes of the consultation.

2.06 Referral for Services

(a) Social workers should refer clients to other professionals when the other professionals' specialized knowledge or expertise is needed to serve clients fully or when social workers believe that they are not being effective or making reasonable progress with clients and that additional service is required.

(b) Social workers who refer clients to other professionals should take appropriate steps to facilitate an orderly transfer of responsibility. Social workers who refer clients to other professionals should disclose, with clients' consent, all pertinent information to the new service providers.

(c) Social workers are prohibited from giving or receiving payment for a referral when no professional service is provided by the referring social worker.

2.07 Sexual Relationships

(a) Social workers who function as supervisors or educators should not engage in sexual activities or contact with supervisees, students, trainees, or other colleagues over whom they exercise professional authority.

(b) Social workers should avoid engaging in sexual relationships with colleagues when there is potential for a conflict of interest. Social workers who become involved in, or anticipate becoming involved in, a sexual relationship with a colleague have a duty to transfer professional responsibilities, when necessary, to avoid a conflict of interest.

2.08 Sexual Harassment

Social workers should not sexually harass supervisees, students, trainees, or colleagues. Sexual harassment includes sexual advances, sexual solicitation, requests for sexual favors, and other verbal or physical conduct of a sexual nature.

2.09 Impairment of Colleagues

(a) Social workers who have direct knowledge of a social work colleague's impairment that is due to personal problems, psychosocial distress, substance abuse, or mental health difficulties and that interferes with practice effectiveness should consult with that colleague when feasible and assist the colleague in taking remedial action.

(b) Social workers who believe that a social work colleague's impairment interferes with practice effectiveness and that the colleague has not taken adequate steps to address the impairment should take action through appropriate channels established by employers, agencies, NASW, licensing and regulatory bodies, and other professional organizations.

2.10 Incompetence of Colleagues

(a) Social workers who have direct knowledge of a social work colleague's incompetence should consult with that colleague when feasible and assist the colleague in taking remedial action.

(b) Social workers who believe that a social work colleague is incompetent and has not taken adequate steps to address the incompetence should take action through appropriate channels established by employers, agencies, NASW, licensing and regulatory bodies, and other professional organizations.

2.11 Unethical Conduct of Colleagues

(a) Social workers should take adequate measures to discourage, prevent, expose, and correct the unethical conduct of colleagues.

(b) Social workers should be knowledgeable about established policies and procedures for handling concerns about colleagues' unethical behavior. Social workers should be familiar with national, state, and local procedures for handling ethics complaints. These include policies and procedures created by NASW, licensing and regulatory bodies, employers, agencies, and other professional organizations.

(c) Social workers who believe that a colleague has acted unethically should seek resolution by discussing their concerns with the colleague when feasible and when such discussion is likely to be productive.

(d) When necessary, social workers who believe that a colleague has acted unethically should take action through appropriate formal channels (such as contacting a state licensing board or regulatory body, an NASW committee on inquiry, or other professional ethics committees).

(e) Social workers should defend and assist colleagues who are unjustly charged with unethical conduct.

3. SOCIAL WORKERS' ETHICAL RESPONSIBILITIES IN PRACTICE SETTINGS

3.01 Supervision and Consultation

(a) Social workers who provide supervision or consultation should have the necessary knowledge and skill to supervise or consult appropriately and should do so only within their areas of knowledge and competence.

(b) Social workers who provide supervision or consultation are responsible for setting clear, appropriate, and culturally sensitive boundaries.

(c) Social workers should not engage in any dual or multiple relationships with supervisees in which there is a risk of exploitation of or potential harm to the supervisee.

(d) Social workers who provide supervision should evaluate supervisees' performance in a manner that is fair and respectful.

3.02 Education and Training

(a) Social workers who function as educators, field instructors for students, or trainers should provide instruction only within their areas of knowledge and competence and should provide instruction based on the most current information and knowledge available in the profession.

(b) Social workers who function as educators or field instructors for students should evaluate students' performance in a manner that is fair and respectful.

(c) Social workers who function as educators or field instructors for students should take reasonable steps to ensure that clients are routinely informed when services are being provided by students.

(d) Social workers who function as educators or field instructors for students should not engage in any dual or multiple relationships with students in which there is a risk of exploitation or potential harm to the student. Social work educators and field instructors are responsible for setting clear, appropriate, and culturally sensitive boundaries.

3.03 Performance Evaluation

Social workers who have responsibility for evaluating the performance of others should fulfill such responsibility in a fair and considerate manner and on the basis of clearly stated criteria.

3.04 Client Records

(a) Social workers should take reasonable steps to ensure that documentation in records is accurate and reflects the services provided.

(b) Social workers should include sufficient and timely documentation in records to facilitate the delivery of services and to ensure continuity of services provided to clients in the future.

(c) Social workers' documentation should protect clients' privacy to the extent that is possible and appropriate and should include only information that is directly relevant to the delivery of services.

(d) Social workers should store records following the termination of services to ensure reasonable future access. Records should be maintained for the number of years required by state statutes or relevant contracts.

3.05 Billing

Social workers should establish and maintain billing practices that accurately reflect the nature and extent of services provided and that identify who provided the service in the practice setting.

3.06 Client Transfer

(a) When an individual who is receiving services from another agency or colleague contacts a social worker for services, the social worker should carefully consider the client's needs before agreeing to provide services. To minimize possible confusion and conflict, social workers should discuss with potential clients the nature of the clients' current relationship with other service providers and the implications, including possible benefits or risks, of entering into a relationship with a new service provider.

(b) If a new client has been served by another agency or colleague, social workers should discuss with the client whether consultation with the previous service provider is in the client's best interest.

3.07 Administration

(a) Social work administrators should advocate within and outside their agencies for adequate resources to meet clients' needs.

(b) Social workers should advocate for resource allocation procedures that are open and fair. When not all clients' needs can be met, an allocation procedure should be developed that is nondiscriminatory and based on appropriate and consistently applied principles.

(c) Social workers who are administrators should take reasonable steps to ensure that adequate agency or organizational resources are available to provide appropriate staff supervision.

(d) Social work administrators should take reasonable steps to ensure that the working environment for which they are responsible is consistent with and encourages compliance with the *NASW Code of Ethics*. Social work administrators should take reasonable steps to eliminate any conditions in their organizations that violate, interfere with, or discourage compliance with the *Code*.

3.08 Continuing Education and Staff Development

Social work administrators and supervisors should take reasonable steps to provide or arrange for continuing education and staff development for all staff for whom they are responsible. Continuing education and staff development should address current knowledge and emerging developments related to social work practice and ethics.

3.09 Commitments to Employers

(a) Social workers generally should adhere to commitments made to employers and employing organizations.

(b) Social workers should work to improve employing agencies' policies and procedures and the efficiency and effectiveness of their services.

(c) Social workers should take reasonable steps to ensure that employers are aware of social workers' ethical obligations as set forth in the *NASW Code of Ethics* and of the implications of those obligations for social work practice.

(d) Social workers should not allow an employing organization's policies, procedures, regulations, or administrative orders to interfere with their ethical practice of social work. Social workers should take reasonable steps to ensure that their employing organizations' practices are consistent with the *NASW Code of Ethics*.

(e) Social workers should act to prevent and eliminate discrimination in the employing organization's work assignments and in its employment policies and practices.

(f) Social workers should accept employment or arrange student field placements only in organizations that exercise fair personnel practices.

(g) Social workers should be diligent stewards of the resources of their employing organizations, wisely conserving funds where appropriate and never misappropriating funds or using them for unintended purposes.

3.10 Labor–Management Disputes

(a) Social workers may engage in organized action, including the formation of and participation in labor unions, to improve services to clients and working conditions.

(b) The actions of social workers who are involved in labor–management disputes, job actions, or labor strikes should be guided by the profession's values, ethical principles, and ethical standards. Reasonable differences of opinion exist among social workers concerning their primary obligation as professionals during an actual or threatened labor strike or job action. Social workers should carefully examine relevant issues and their possible impact on clients before deciding on a course of action.

4.   SOCIAL WORKERS' ETHICAL RESPONSIBILITIES AS PROFESSIONALS

4.01 Competence

(a) Social workers should accept responsibility or employment only on the basis of existing competence or the intention to acquire the necessary competence.

(b) Social workers should strive to become and remain proficient in professional practice and the performance of professional functions. Social workers should critically examine and keep current with emerging knowledge relevant to social work. Social workers should routinely review the professional literature and participate in continuing education relevant to social work practice and social work ethics.

(c) Social workers should base practice on recognized knowledge, including empirically based knowledge, relevant to social work and social work ethics.

4.02 Discrimination

Social workers should not practice, condone, facilitate, or collaborate with any form of discrimination on the basis of race, ethnicity, national origin, color, sex, sexual orientation, age, marital status, political belief, religion, or mental or physical disability.

4.03 Private Conduct

Social workers should not permit their private conduct to interfere with their ability to fulfill their professional responsibilities.

4.04 Dishonesty, Fraud, and Deception

Social workers should not participate in, condone, or be associated with dishonesty, fraud, or deception.

4.05 Impairment

(a) Social workers should not allow their own personal problems, psychosocial distress, legal problems, substance abuse, or mental health difficulties to interfere with their professional judgment and performance or to jeopardize the best interests of people for whom they have a professional responsibility.

(b) Social workers whose personal problems, psychosocial distress, legal problems, substance abuse, or mental health difficulties interfere with their professional judgment and performance should immediately seek consultation and take appropriate remedial action by seeking professional help, making adjustments in workload, terminating practice, or taking any other steps necessary to protect clients and others.

4.06 Misrepresentation

(a) Social workers should make clear distinctions between statements made and actions engaged in as a private individual and as a representative of the social work profession, a professional social work organization, or the social worker's employing agency.

(b) Social workers who speak on behalf of professional social work organizations should accurately represent the official and authorized positions of the organizations.

(c) Social workers should ensure that their representations to clients, agencies, and the public of professional qualifications, credentials, education, competence, affiliations, services provided, or results to be achieved are accurate. Social workers should claim only those relevant professional credentials they actually possess and take steps to correct any inaccuracies or misrepresentations of their credentials by others.

4.07 Solicitations

(a) Social workers should not engage in uninvited solicitation of potential clients who, because of their circumstances, are vulnerable to undue influence, manipulation, or coercion.

(b) Social workers should not engage in solicitation of testimonial endorsements (including solicitation of consent to use a client's prior statement as a testimonial endorsement) from current clients or from other people who, because of their particular circumstances, are vulnerable to undue influence.

4.08 Acknowledging Credit

(a) Social workers should take responsibility and credit, including authorship credit, only for work they have actually performed and to which they have contributed.

(b) Social workers should honestly acknowledge the work of and the contributions made by others.

5. SOCIAL WORKERS' ETHICAL RESPONSIBILITIES TO THE SOCIAL WORK PROFESSION

5.01 Integrity of the Profession

(a) Social workers should work toward the maintenance and promotion of high standards of practice.

(b) Social workers should uphold and advance the values, ethics, knowledge, and mission of the profession. Social workers should protect, enhance, and improve the integrity of the profession through appropriate study and research, active discussion, and responsible criticism of the profession.

(c) Social workers should contribute time and professional expertise to activities that promote respect for the value, integrity, and competence of the social work profession. These activities may include teaching, research, consultation, service, legislative testimony, presentations in the community, and participation in their professional organizations.

(d) Social workers should contribute to the knowledge base of social work and share with colleagues their knowledge related to practice, research, and ethics. Social workers should seek to con-tribute to the profession's literature and to share their knowledge at professional meetings and conferences.

(e) Social workers should act to prevent the unauthorized and unqualified practice of social work.

5.02 Evaluation and Research

(a) Social workers should monitor and evaluate policies, the implementation of programs, and practice interventions.

(b) Social workers should promote and facilitate evaluation and research to contribute to the development of knowledge.

(c) Social workers should critically examine and keep current with emerging knowledge relevant to social work and fully use evaluation and research evidence in their professional practice.

(d) Social workers engaged in evaluation or research should carefully consider possible consequences and should follow guidelines developed for the protection of evaluation and research participants. Appropriate institutional review boards should be consulted.

(e) Social workers engaged in evaluation or research should obtain voluntary and written informed consent from participants, when appropriate, without any implied or actual deprivation or penalty for refusal to participate; without undue inducement to participate; and with due regard for participants' well-being, privacy, and dignity. Informed consent should include information about the nature, extent, and duration of the participation requested and disclosure of the risks and benefits of participation in the research.

(f) When evaluation or research participants are incapable of giving informed consent, social workers should provide an appropriate explanation to the participants, obtain the participants' assent to the extent they are able, and obtain written consent from an appropriate proxy.

(g) Social workers should never design or conduct evaluation or research that does not use consent procedures, such as certain forms of naturalistic observation and archival research, unless rigorous and responsible review of the research has found it to be justified because of its prospective scientific, educational, or applied value and unless equally effective alternative procedures that do not involve waiver of consent are not feasible.

(h) Social workers should inform participants of their right to withdraw from evaluation and research at any time without penalty.

(i) Social workers should take appropriate steps to ensure that participants in evaluation and research have access to appropriate supportive services.

(j) Social workers engaged in evaluation or research should protect participants from unwarranted physical or mental distress, harm, danger, or deprivation.

(k) Social workers engaged in the evaluation of services should discuss collected information only for professional purposes and only with people professionally concerned with this information.

(l) Social workers engaged in evaluation or research should ensure the anonymity or confidentiality of participants and of the data obtained from them. Social workers should inform participants of any limits of confidentiality, the measures that will be taken to ensure confidentiality, and when any records containing research data will be destroyed.

(m) Social workers who report evaluation and research results should protect participants' confidentiality by omitting identifying information unless proper consent has been obtained authorizing disclosure.

(n) Social workers should report evaluation and research findings accurately. They should not fabricate or falsify results and should take steps to correct any errors later found in published data using standard publication methods.

(o) Social workers engaged in evaluation or research should be alert to and avoid conflicts of interest and dual relationships with participants, should inform participants when a real or potential conflict of interest arises, and should take steps to resolve the issue in a manner that makes participants' interests primary.

(p) Social workers should educate themselves, their students, and their colleagues about responsible research practices.

6.   SOCIAL WORKERS' ETHICAL RESPONSIBILITIES TO THE BROADER SOCIETY

6.01 Social Welfare

Social workers should promote the general welfare of society, from local to global levels, and the development of people, their communities, and their environments. Social workers should advocate for living conditions conducive to the fulfillment of basic human needs and should promote social, economic, political, and cultural values and institutions that are compatible with the realization of social justice.

6.02 Public Participation

Social workers should facilitate informed participation by the public in shaping social policies and institutions.

6.03 Public Emergencies

Social workers should provide appropriate professional services in public emergencies to the greatest extent possible.

6.04 Social and Political Action

(a) Social workers should engage in social and political action that seeks to ensure that all people have equal access to the resources, employment, services, and opportunities they require to meet their basic human needs and to develop fully. Social workers should be aware of the impact of the political arena on practice and should advocate for changes in policy and legislation to improve social conditions in order to meet basic human needs and promote social justice.

(b) Social workers should act to expand choice and opportunity for all people, with special regard for vulnerable, disadvantaged, oppressed, and exploited people and groups.

(c) Social workers should promote conditions that encourage respect for cultural and social diversity within the United States and globally. Social workers should promote policies and practices that demonstrate respect for difference, support the expansion of cultural knowledge and resources, advocate for programs and institutions that demonstrate cultural competence, and promote policies that safeguard the rights of and confirm equity and social justice for all people.

(d) Social workers should act to prevent and eliminate domination of, exploitation of, and discrimination against any person, group, or class on the basis of race, ethnicity, national origin, color, sex, sexual orientation, age, marital status, political belief, religion, or mental or physical disability.

APPENDIX B.

Category of Feeling

Level of Intensity	Happiness	Sadness	Fear	Uncertainty	Anger	Strength, potency	Weakness, inadequacy
Strong	Excited	Despairing	Panicked	Bewildered	Outraged	Powerful	Ashamed
	Thrilled	Hopeless	Terrified	Disoriented	Hostile	Authoritative	Powerless
	Delighted	Depressed	Afraid	Mistrustful	Furious	Forceful	Vulnerable
	Overjoyed	Crushed	Frightened	Confused	Angry	Potent	Cowardly
	Ecstatic	Miserable	Scared		Harsh		Exhausted
	Elated	Abandoned	Overwhelmed		Hateful		Impotent
	Jubilant	Defeated			Mean		
		Desolate			Vindictive		
Moderate	"Up"	Dejected	Worried	Doubtful	Aggravated	Tough	Embarrassed
	Good	Dismayed	Shaky	Mixed up	Irritated	Important	Useless
	Happy	Disillusioned	Tense	Insecure	Offended	Confident	Demoralized
	Optimistic	Lonely	Anxious	Skeptical	Mad	Fearless	Helpless
	Cheerful	Bad	Threatened	Puzzled	Frustrated	Energetic	Worn out
	Enthusiastic	Unhappy	Agitated		Resentful	Brave	Inept
	Joyful	Pessimistic			"Sore"	Courageous	Incapable
	"Turned on"	Sad			Upset	Daring	Incompetent
		Hurt			Impatient	Assured	Inadequate
		Lost			Obstinate	Adequate	Shaken
						Self-confident	
						Skillful	
Weak	Pleased	"Down"	Jittery	Unsure	Perturbed	Determined	Frail
	Glad	Discouraged	Jumpy	Surprised	Annoyed	Firm	Meek
	Content	Disappointed	Nervous	Uncertain	Grouchy	Able	Unable
	Relaxed	"Blue"	Edgy	Undecided	Hassled	Strong	Weak
	Satisfied	Alone	Uptight	Bothered	Bothered		
	Calm	Left out	Uneasy		Disagreeable		
			Defensive				
			Apprehensive				
			Hesitant				
			Uncomfortable				

Adapted from *The Skills of Helping*, by R.R. Carkhuff and W.A. Anthony. (1997).

APPENDIX C.

Multimodal Life History Questionnaire*

PURPOSE OF THIS QUESTIONNAIRE:

The purpose of this questionnaire is to obtain a comprehensive picture of your background. In psychotherapy, records are necessary, since they permit a more thorough dealing with one's problems. By completing these questions as fully and as accurately as you can, you will facilitate your therapeutic program. You are requested to answer these routine questions in your own time instead of using up your actual consulting time. It is understandable that you might be concerned about what happens to the information about you because much or all of this information is highly personal. Case records are strictly confidential. **NO OUTSIDER IS PERMITTED TO SEE YOUR CASE RECORD WITHOUT YOUR PERMISSION.**

If you do not desire to answer any questions, merely write, "Do Not Care to Answer."

Date: _____

1.   General Information:

Name: _____

Address: _____

_____

Telephone Numbers: (days) _____ (evenings) _____

Age: _____   Occupation _____ Sex _____

By whom were you referred? _____

Marital Status (cricle one): Single   Engaged   Married   Separated   Divorced   Widowed

Remarried (how many tmes? _____ Living with someone_____

Do you live in: house, hotel, room, apartment _____

2.   Description of Presenting Problems:

State in your own words the nature of your main problems _____

_____

_____

_____

_____

_____

_____

On the scale below please estimate the severity of your problem(s):

Mildly   Moderately   Very   Extremely   Totally

Upsetting_____Upsetting_____Severe_____Severe_____Incapacitating_____

When did your problems being (give dates):_____

_____

_____

_____

_____

The Multimodal Life History Questionnaire by Arnold Lazarus. Copyright © 1980 by the Multimodal Therapy Institute. Reprinted by permission.

Please describe significant events occurring at that time, or since then, which may relate to the development or maintenance of your problems: _____
_____

What solutions to your problems have been most helpful? _____
_____

Have you been in therapy before or received any prior professional assistance for your problems? If so, please give name(s), professional titles(s), dates of treatments and results:_____
_____

3.   Personal and Social History
(a)   Date of Birth _____Place of Birth _____
(b)   Siblings: Number of Brothers _____ Brothers' Ages: _____
                 Number of Sisters _____ Sisters' Ages: _____
(c)   Father: Living? _____ If alive, give father's age _____
                 Deceased? _____ If deceased, give his age at time of death _____
                      How old were you at the time? _____
                 Cause of Death _____
                 Occupation _____ Health _____
(d)   Mother: Living? _____ If alive, give mother's age _____
                 Deceased? _____ If deceased, give her age at time of death _____
                      How old were you at the time? _____
                 Cause of Death _____
                 Occupation _____ Health _____
(e)   Religion: As a Child: _____ As an Adult: _____
(f)   Education: What is the last grade completed (degree)? _____
(g)   Scholastic Strengths and Weaknesses: _____
_____

(h)   Underline any of the following that applied during your childhood/adolescence:
Happy Childhood   School Problems   Medical Problems
Unhappy Childhood   Family Problems   Alcohol Abuse
Emotional/Behavior Problems   Strong Religious   Convictions
Legal Trouble   Drug Abuse   Others:

(i)   What sort of work are you doing now? _____
(j)   What kinds of jobs have you held in the past? _____
_____

(k)   Does your present work satisfy you? If not, please explain_____
_____
(l)   What is your annual family income? _____ How much
does it cost you to live? _____
(m)   What were your past ambitions? _____
_____
(n)   What are your current ambitions? _____
_____
(o)   What is your height? _____ ft. _____ inches   What is your weight? _____ lbs.
(p)   Have you ever been hospitalized for psychological problems? Yes _____ No _____
If yes, when and where? _____
(q)   Do you have a family physician? Yes _____ No _____ If so, please give his/her name(s)
        and telephone number(s) _____

(r)   Have you ever attempted suicide? Yes _____ No _____
(s)   Does any member of your family suffer from alcoholism, epilepsy, depression or anything else
        that might be considered a "mental disorder?" _____
(t)   Has any relative attempted or committed suicide? _____
(u)   Has any relative had serious problems with the "law?" _____

Modality Analysis of Current Problems

The following section is designed to help you describe your current problems in greater detail and to identify problems which might otherwise go unnoticed. This will enable us to design a comprehensive treatment program and tailor it to your specific needs. The following section is organized according to the seven (7) modalities of *Behavior, Feelings, Physical Sensations, Images, Thoughts, Interpersonal Relationships* and *Biological Factors*.

4.   Behavior

Underline any of the following behaviors that apply to you:

Overeat	Suicidal attempts	Can't keep a job
Take drugs	Compulsions	Insomnia
Vomiting	Smoke	Take too many risks
Odd behavior	Withdrawal	Lazy
Drink too much	Nervous tics	Eating problems
Work too hard	Concentration difficulties	Aggressive behavior
Procrastination	Sleep disturbance	Crying
Impulsive reactions	Phobic avoidance	Outbursts of temper

Are there any specific behaviors, actions or habits that you would like to change? _____
_____
What are some special talents or skills that you feel proud of? _____
_____
What would you like to do more of? _____
What would you like to do less of? _____
What would you like to start doing? _____
What would you like to stop doing? _____
How is your free time spent? _____
_____

Do you keep yourself compulsively busy doing an endless list of chores or meaningless activities? _____
Do you practice relaxation or meditation regularly? _____

5. Feelings

Underline any of the following feelings that often apply to you:

Angry	Guilty	Unhappy
Annoyed	Happy	Bored
Sad	Conflicted	Restless
Depressed	Regretful	Lonely
Anxious	Hopeless	Contented
Fearful	Hopeful	Excited
Panicky	Helpless	Optimistic
Energetic	Relaxed	Tense
Envious	Jealous	Others:

List your five main fears:

1.
2.
3.
4.
5.

What feelings would you most like to experience more often? _____

What feelings would you like to experience less often?_____

What are some positive feelings you have experienced recently?_____

When are you most likely to lose control of your feeling?_____

Describe any situations that make you feel calm or relaxed?_____

_____

_____

Please complete the following:

If I told you what I'm feeling now _____

One of the things I feel proud of is _____

One of the things I feel guilty about is _____

I am happiest when _____

One of the things that saddens me the most is _____

If I weren't afraid to be myself, I might _____

I get so angry when _____

If I get angry with you _____

What kinds of hobbies or leisure activities do you enjoy or find relaxing?

_____

Do you have trouble relaxing and enjoying weekends and vacations? (If "yes," please explain)

_____

6. Physical Sensations:

Underline any of the following that often apply to you:

Headaches	Stomach trouble	Skin problems
Dizziness	Tics	Dry mouth
Palpitations	Fatigue	Burning or itchy skin
Muscle spasms	Twitches	Chest pains
Tension	Back pain	Rapid heart beat
Sexual disturbances	Tremors	Don't like being touched
Unable to relax	Fainting spells	Blackouts
Bowel disturbances	Hear things	Excessive sweating
Tingling	Watery eyes	Visual disturbances
Numbness	Flushes	Hearing problems

MENSTRUAL HISTORY:

Age of first period _____ Were you informed or did it come as a shock? _____

Are you regular? _____ Date of last period _____

Duration _____Do you have pain? _____

Do your periods affect your mood? _____

What sensations are especially:

Pleasant for you? _____

_____

Unpleasant for you? _____

_____

7. Images

Underline any of the following that apply to you:

Pleasant sexual images	Unpleasant sexual images
Unpleasant childhood images	Lonely images
Helpless images	Seduction images
Aggressive images	Images of being loved

Check which of the following applies to you:

I PICTURE MYSELF:

being hurt	hurting others
not coping	being in charge
succeeding	failing
losing control	being trapped
being followed	being laughed at
being talked about	being promiscuous
others:	

What picture comes to into your mind most often?

Describe a very pleasant image, mental picture, or fantasy.

Describe a very unpleasant image picture, or fantasy.

Describe your image of a completely "safe place."

How often do you have nightmares?

8.   Thoughts:

Underline each of the following thoughts that apply to you:

I am worthless nobody, useless and/or unlovable.
I am unattractive, incompetent, stupid and/or undesirable.
I am evil, crazy, degenerate, and/or deviant.
Life is empty, a waste; there is nothing to look forward to.
I make too many mistakes, can't do anything right.

Underline each of the following words that you might use to describe yourself:

Intelligent, confident, worthwhile, ambitious, sensitive, loyal, trustworthy, full of regrets, worthless, a nobody useless, evil crazy, morally, degenerate, considerate, deviant, unattractive, unlovable, inadequate, confused, ugly, stupid, naïve, honest, incompetent, horrible thoughts, conflicted, concentration difficulties, memory problems, attractive, can't make decisions, suicidal, persevering, good sense of humor, hard-working.

What do you consider to be your most irrational thought or idea?

Are you bothered by thoughts that occur over and over again?

On each of the following items, please circle the number that most reflects your opinions:

	STRONGLY DISAGREE	DISAGREE	NEUTRAL	AGREE	STRONGLY AGREE
I should not make mistakes	1	2	3	4	5
I should be good at everything I do.	1	2	3	4	5
When I do not know, I should pretend that I do.	1	2	3	4	5
I should not disclose personal information.	1	2	3	4	5
I am a victim of circumstances.	1	2	3	4	5
My life is controlled by outside forces.	1	2	3	4	5
Other people are happier than I am.	1	2	3	4	5
It is very important to please other people.	1	2	3	4	5
Play it safe: don't take any risk.	1	2	3	4	5
I don't deserve to be happy.	1	2	3	4	5
If I ignore my problems, they will go away.	1	2	3	4	5
It is my responsibility to make other people happy.	1	2	3	4	5
I should strive for perfection.	1	2	3	4	5
Basically, there are two ways of doing things ---the right way and the wrong way.	1	2	3	4	5

Expectations regarding therapy:

In a few words what do you think therapy is all about?

How long do you think your therapy should last?

How do you think a therapist should interact with his or her clients? What personal qualities do you think the ideal therapist should posses?

(Please complete the following:)
I am a person who _____
All my life _____
Ever since I was a child _____
It's hard for me to admit _____
One of the things I can't forgive is _____
A good thing about having problems is _____
The bad thing about growing up is _____
One of the ways I could help myself but don't is _____

9. Interpersonal Relationships

A. Family of Origin

(1) If you were not bought up by your parents who raised you and between what years?
(2) Give a description of your father (or father substitute's) personality and his attitude toward you (past and present):
(3) Give a description of your mother (or mother substitute's) personality and her attitude toward you (past and present):
(4) In what ways were you disciplined (punished) by your parents as a child?
(5) Give an impression of your home atmosphere (i.e., the home in which you grew up). Mention state of compatibility between parents and between children.
(6) Were you able to confide in your parents?
(7) Did your parents understand you?
(8) Basically, did you feel loved and respected by your parents?
(9) If you have a step-parent, give your age when parent remarried.
(10) Has anyone (parents, relatives, friends0 ever interfered in your marriage, occupation, etc.?
(11) Who are the most important people in your life?

B. Friendships
(1) Do you make friends easily?
(2) Do you keep them?
(3) Were you ever bullied or severely teased?
(4) Describe any relationship that gives you :
   (a) Joy

   (b) Grief

(5) Rate the degree to which you generally feel comfortable and relaxed in social situations:
   Very relaxed____ Relatively comfortable____ Relatively uncomfortable____ Very anxious____

(6) Generally, do you express your feelings, opinions, and wishes to others in the open appropriate manner? Describe those individuals with whom (or those situations in which) you have trouble asserting yourself?

(7) Did you date much in High School? College?

(8) Do have one or more friends with whom you feel comfortable sharing your most private thoughts and feeling?

C. Marriage:
(1) How long did you know your spouse before your engagement?
(2) How long have you been married?
(3) What is your spouse's age?
(4) What is your spouse's occupation?
(5) Describe your spouse's personality.

(6) In what areas are you compatible?

(7) In what areas are you incompatible?

(8) How do you get along with your in-laws (this includes brothers and sisters-in-law)?

(9) How many children do you have? _____ Please give their names, ages and sexes:

(10) Do any of your children present special problems?
(11) Any relevant information regarding abortions or miscarriages?

D. Sexual Relationships:

(1) Describe your parents' attitude toward sex. Was sex discussed in your home?

(2) When and how did you derive your first knowledge of sex?

(3) When did you first become aware of your own sexual impulses?

(4) Have you ever experienced any anxiety or guilt feelings arising out of sex or masturbation? If yes, please explain.

(5) Any relevant details regarding your first or subsequent sexual experiences?

(6) Is your present sex life satisfactory? If not, please explain.

(7) Provide information about any significant homosexual reactions or relationships.

(8) Please note any sexual concerns not discussed above.

E. Other Relationships

(1) Are there any problems in your relationships with people at work? If so, please describe.

(2) Please complete the following:
     (a) One of the ways people hurt me is _____

     _____

     (b) I could shock you by _____

     _____

     (c) A mother should _____

     _____

     (d) A father should _____

     _____

     (e) A true friend should _____

     _____

(3) Give a brief description of yourself as you would be described by:
     (a) Your spouse (if married):

     (b) Your best friend:

     (c) Some who dislikes you:

(4) Are you currently troubled by any past rejections or loss of a love relationship? If so, please explain.

10.   Biological Factors:

Do you have any current concerns about your physical health? Please specify:

_____

Please list any medicines you are currently taking, or have taken during the past 6 months (including aspirin, birth control pills, or any medicines that were prescribed or taken over the counter) _____

_____

Do you eat three well-balanced meals each day? If not, please explain.

_____

Do you get regular physical exercise? If so, what type and how often?

_____

Check any of the following that apply to you:

	NEVER	RARELY	FREQUENTLY	VERY OFTEN
Marijuana				
Tranquilizers				
Sedatives				
Aspirin				
Cocaine				
Painkillers				
Alcohol				
Coffee				
Cigarettes				
Narcotics				
Stimulants				
Hallucinogens (LSD, etc.)				
Diarrhea				

	NEVER	RARELY	FREQUENTLY	VERY OFTEN

Constipation _____
Allergies _____
High blood pressure _____
Heart problems_____
Nausea _____
Vomiting _____
Insomnia _____
Headaches _____
Backache _____
Early morning awakening _____
Fitful sleep _____
Overeat _____
Poor appetite _____
Eat "junk foods" _____

Underline any of the following that apply to you or members of your family; thyroid disease, kidney disease, asthma, neurological disease, infectious diseases, diabetes, cancer, gastrointestinal disease, prostate problems, glaucoma, epilepsy, other:

Have you ever had any head injuries or loss of consciousness? Please give details. _____
_____

Please describe any surgery you have had (give dates) _____
_____

Please describe any accidents or injuries you have suffered (give dates) _____
_____

Sequential History
Please outline your most significant memories and experiences within the following ages:
0-5 _____
6-10 _____
11-15 _____
16-20 _____
21-25 _____
26-30 _____
31-35 _____
36-40 _____
41-45 _____
46-50 _____
51-55 _____
56-60 _____
61-65 _____

REFERENCES

American Psychiatric Association. (1994). *Diagnostic and statistical manual of mental disorders*, 4th ed. Washington, DC: American Psychiatric Association.

Ashford, J., Lecroy, C., and Lortie, K. (1997). *Human behavior in the social environment*. Pacific Grove, CA: Brooks/Cole.

Atkinson, D., Morten, G., and Sue, D. (1998). *Counseling American minorities*, 5th ed. Boston, MA: McGraw-Hill.

Bibb, A. and Casimir, G. (1996). Haitian families. In Monica McGoldrick, Joe Giordano, and John K. Pearce (Eds.), *Ethnicity and family therapy* (pp. 86-111). New York: Guilford.

Comas-Diaz, L. and Greene, B. (1994). Overview: An ethnocultural mosaic. In L. Comas-Diaz and B. Greene (Eds.) *Women of color: Integrating ethnic and gender identities in psychotherapy*. New York: Guilford.

Cormier, W. and Cormier, S. (1991). *Interviewing strategies for helpers*, 3rd ed. Pacific Grove, CA: Brooks/Cole.

DeAndre, D. (1984). Bicultural socialization: Factors affecting minority experience. *Social Work 29*, 172-181.

De Jong, P. and Miller, S. (1995). How to interview for client strengths. *Social Work Journal 40*(6), 729-736.

Egan, G. (1997). *The skilled helper*, 6th ed. Pacific Grove, CA: Brooks/Cole.

Ehrenreich, J. H. (1985). *The Altruistic Imagination*. Ithaca, NY: Cornell University Press.

Germaine, C., and Gitterman, A. (1996). *The life model of social work practice*. New York: Columbia University Press.

Gothard, S. (1997). Legal issues: Confidentiality and privileged communication. In National Association of Social Workers Encyclopedia of Social Work, 19th ed. Washington, DC: NASW.

Haynes, K. S. and Holmes, K. A. (1994). *Invitation to Social Work*. New York: Longman.

Hepworth, D., Rooney, R., and Larsen, J. (1997). *Direct Social Work Practice: Theory and skills*, 5th ed. Pacific Grove, CA: Brooks/Cole.

Hines, P and Boyd-Franklin, N. (1996). African American families. In Monica McGoldrick, Joe Giordano, and John K. Pearce (Eds.), *Ethnicity and family therapy* (pp. 66-84). New York: Guilford.

Kadushin, A. and Kadushin, G. (1997). *The social work interview*, 4th ed. New York: Columbia University Press.

Lee, E. (1996). Chinese families. In Monica McGoldrick, Joe Giordano, and John K. Pearce (Eds.), *Ethnicity and family therapy* (pp. 249-267). New York: Guilford.

Leung, P and Boehnlein, J. (1996). Vietnamese families. In Monica McGoldrick, Joe Giordano, and John K. Pearce (Eds.), *Ethnicity and family therapy* (pp. 295-306). New York: Guilford.

Levy, C. (1973). The value base of social work. *Journal of Education for Social Work. 9*, 34-42.

Levy, C. (1976). *Social Work Ethics*. New York: Human Sciences Press.

Madrigal, C. (1995). The AIDS crisis in the Latino(a) community. Paper presented at the annual meetings of the Midwest Sociological Society, Chicago, IL, April 6-9.

McGoldrick, M. (1996). Irish families. In Monica McGoldrick, Joe Giordano, and John K. Pearce (Eds.), *Ethnicity and family therapy* (pp. 544-566). New York: Guilford.

Minahan, A. (1981). Purpose and objectives of social work revisited. *Social Work, 26*(1), 5-6.

Murphy, B. and Dillon, C. (1998). *Interviewing in action: Process and practice*. Pacific Grove, CA: Brooks/Cole.

National Association of Social Workers (1981). *NASW standards for the classification of social work practice.*   Washington, DC: NASW.

National Association of Social Workers (1997). *Encyclopedia of Social Work,* 19th ed. Washington, DC: NASW.

Perlman H. H. (1976). Believing and doing: Values in social work education. *Social Casework,* 7(6), 381-390.

Polowy, C. I. and Gorenberg, C. (1997). Legal issues: Recent developments in confidentiality and privilege. In National Association of Social Workers *Encyclopedia of Social Work,* 19th ed. Washington, DC: NASW.

Queralt, M. (1996). *The social environment and human behavior: A diversity perspective.* Boston, MA: Allyn & Bacon.

Reamer, F.G. (1995). *Social Work Values and Ethics.* New York: Columbia University Press.

Reamer, F.G. (1997a).Ethics and values. In National Association of Social Workers Encyclopedia of Social Work, 19th ed. Washington, DC: NASW.

Reamer, F.G. (1997b). Ethical standards in social work: The *NASW Code of Ethics.* In National Association of Social Workers, *Encyclopedia of Social Work* 19th ed. Washington, DC: NASW.

Sheafor, B., Horejsi, C. and Horejsi, G. (1997). *Techniques and guidelines for social work practice,* 4th ed. Boston, MA: Allyn & Bacon.

Zastrow, C. (1995). *The Practice of Social Work.* Pacific Grove, CA: Brooks/Cole Publishing Company.

Zastrow, C. and Kirst-Ashman, K. (1990). *Understanding human behavior and the social environment,* 2nd ed. Chicago, IL: Nelson-Hall.

NOTES

NOTES

NOTES

NOTES

NOTES

NOTES

NOTES

NOTES

NOTES

NOTES